MAKING RELATIONAL CARE WORK FOR OLDER PEOPLE

This book explores the concept of relational care, what it feels like for older people and for carers, why it makes life happier and how those involved in residential or community care can make it work.

Relational care is gaining traction as its benefits to individuals and society become recognised. This accessible book, based on real-life models and in-depth interviews, explores fresh ways that relational care can be facilitated in a variety of settings. It looks at practice in terms of team management, support for care workers, technology, design and architecture, intergenerational and multidisciplinary models, and their implications for resilience, wellbeing, policy and future funding. Chapters are arranged by theme and provide descriptions, learning points and resources for each model, as well as incorporating a wealth of interviews giving insights into the lived experience of relational care.

This is a lively book full of realistic ideas and information for everyone who wants to find out more about, access or implement the best in care – the best for older people, their families, care workers, management and society.

Jenny Kartupelis started her career in public relations, establishing an award-winning consultancy; she subsequently moved into the charitable sector, helping to set up and becoming Director of a regional interfaith forum, for which she was awarded the MBE for services to interfaith relations. She has been commissioned to undertake extensive survey and analysis work by public- and third-sector bodies, resulting in changes of practice and in policy. Jenny was educated at the Universities of Kent, Sussex and Cambridge and is an advisor to The World Congress of Faiths and Faith in Society Ltd.

MAKING RELATIONAL CARE WORK FOR OLDER PEOPLE

Exploring Innovation and Best Practice in Everyday Life

Jenny Kartupelis

Routledge
Taylor & Francis Group

LONDON AND NEW YORK

First published 2021
by Routledge
2 Park Square, Milton Park, Abingdon, Oxon OX14 4RN

and by Routledge
52 Vanderbilt Avenue, New York, NY 10017

Routledge is an imprint of the Taylor & Francis Group, an informa business

British Library Cataloguing-in-Publication Data
A catalogue record for this book is available from the British Library

Library of Congress Cataloging-in-Publication Data
Names: Kartupelis, Jenny, 1953– author.
Title: Making relational care work for older people: exploring
innovation and best practice in everyday life / Jenny Kartupelis.
Description: New York: Routledge, 2020. |
Includes bibliographical references and index.
Identifiers: LCCN 2020017033 (print) | LCCN 2020017034 (ebook) |
ISBN 9780367366193 (hardback) | ISBN 9780367408541 (paperback) |
ISBN 9780367809454 (ebook)
Subjects: LCSH: Older people—Care. | Social service. | Helping behavior.
Classification: LCC HV1451 .K367 2020 (print) |
LCC HV1451 (ebook) | DDC 362.6—dc23
LC record available at https://lccn.loc.gov/2020017033
LC ebook record available at https://lccn.loc.gov/2020017034

ISBN: 978-0-367-36619-3 (hbk)
ISBN: 978-0-367-40854-1 (pbk)
ISBN: 978-0-367-80945-4 (ebk)

Typeset in Bembo
by codeMantra

CONTENTS

CONTRIBUTOR

Lorraine Morley has a background in open innovation and entrepreneurship research and practice. She is a business owner, researcher and lecturer, with particular expertise in technologies for ageing and longevity. Lorraine leads Age-Tech Accelerator UK – a collaborative programme which scouts for, identifies and supports businesses with innovations for later-life living.

FOREWORD

The experience of ageing varies so much: for some it can be a time of greater contentment and fulfilment; for some it brings a new era of activity and fresh achievement; while for others it may represent a decline in mental and physical wellbeing or a state of loneliness, anxiety and even fear.

Improving that experience, not only of older people but also of those who care for them, should be a mission of civilised society, and one for which I myself have striven over many years: as Director General of Age Concern until 2000, and currently in my position as Co-chair of the All-Party Parliamentary Groups for Ageing and Older People, and for Dementia. I am therefore more than pleased to welcome the arrival of this book, which proposes a new approach to supporting older people to thrive in care environments, both residential and community based.

The concept of 'relational care' as a means to understanding and delivering realistic care models that enable more autonomy, flourishing, life purpose and mutual support for older adults and for care staff has the potential for significant change. Moreover, it is not only possible but is actually happening already in community care teams and care homes around the UK. The author bases her proposition on numerous first-hand interviews, and on her visits to a variety of settings, enabling the voices of older people to be heard directly. In so doing she has garnered an important amount of new information and also helps to address the problems of an almost unconscious ageism that sidelines lived experience in favour of assumptions and accepted lore.

This is a practical and realistic publication, giving insights into innovation, best practice and methods that work and offering learning that can be replicated by organisations committed to improved wellbeing. It argues for fresh thinking by older people themselves; by public, private and third-sector bodies; and by policy makers and funders. I very much hope to see it influence the way social care is delivered in the UK in the future.

Baroness Sally Greengross of Notting Hill OBE

PROLOGUE

My first encounter with Jenny Kartupelis was in 2014 when she led the organisation of a successful Abbeyfield Society interdisciplinary symposium on the theme of 'Spirituality and Older People'. Her presentation at that event reported findings from a survey on wellbeing in care homes. This work demonstrated Jenny's commitment to ethical care and reminded all present of the value of representing the voices of older adults and care-givers in understanding spiritual care. Jenny's experience of leading interfaith relations activity, in the charitable sector and as a champion for holistic care for older adults serves as a strong basis for a book on relational care for older adults.

Jenny Kartupelis states that the purpose of her book 'is to review and present good practice and innovation in creating care environments that work for all involved in them. The intention is not to review and compare good and bad practice but to focus on the best that can be achieved and how to make it happen'. This is a praiseworthy intention and one that is most critical in challenging times. Jenny's intention to illuminate care practices worthy of celebration leads the way in showing how ethical care can be sustained.

Each of the book's six chapters provides material for reflection regarding the meaning, operationalisation and evaluation of relational care. Chapter 1 introduces central concepts such as person-centredness, care ethics, resilience, flourishing and relational care. Chapter 2 focusses on different models of relational care, for example, Neighbourhood Cares, Buurtzorg Teams and Wellbeing teams. Chapter 3 draws on the perspectives of older adults and care-givers regarding relational care, including the important role of environmental factors. Innovations in practice are the focus of Chapter 4, and Jenny draws on data from pioneering organisations which implemented the Montessori approach and intergenerational living. Chapter 5, authored by Lorraine Morley, focusses on the role of technology and discusses some of the opportunities and challenges that arise for relational care. In the final chapter, the future of residential care is considered, and this raises significant ethical questions regarding societal and policy priorities. In the light of the current global pandemic, absorbing all countries at the time of writing, such questions are all the more pressing.

This book draws attention to positive and innovative approaches to the care of older adults, focussing on central role of relationships. The approach to relational care is underpinned by an ethics of care and is strengthened by quotations from older adults and care-givers. It is likely that all who read this book will be heartened and inspired by the positive initiatives detailed in the book. It is hoped that readers will follow Jenny Kartupelis' lead in promoting relationships – and the moral climate of care organisations – that affirm the dignity of older adults, enable them to have a voice and express their individuality so they live as well as possible in their later years.

Ann Gallagher, Professor of Ethics and Care,
International Care Ethics Observatory,
University of Surrey

Ann Gallagher is the author of *Slow Ethics and the Art of*
Gallagher, A. (2020) *Slow Ethics and the Art of Care*, Emerald Publishing.
doi/10.1108/9781839091957

PREFACE

As I write this, the United Kingdom, together with most countries around the world, is in 'lockdown' as a result of the novel coronavirus outbreak, with its peak here expected in a few weeks. It is a strange and somewhat surreal time, and I have naturally been wondering whether and how its aftermath may affect the ideas and information presented in this book. It is impossible to forecast the future, but I believe that the concept and principles of relational care are enduring and, even in changing circumstances, have so much to offer the way we look holistically at the care of older people.

Yesterday I walked into the market town in which I live for some essentials: the streets were near empty, the closed shops and general quietness reminiscent of childhood Sundays. But below these still waters, there is a current of caring that is gathering strength. People are looking out for the wellbeing not just of family and friends but neighbours and strangers. 'Just checking' phone calls and emails are flying around, and after a call by the NHS for 250,000 volunteers, over 700,000 have registered so far. Support and appreciation not only for vital health professionals but for all key workers are near-universal, and perhaps social carers will never again be dismissed as low-skilled or dispensable.

There is more overt acknowledgement that we are all connected: locally, nationally and globally. If a growing recognition that interactions and their consequences – between nature, animals, people and the world – are inescapable, perhaps society can become a happier and more accepting place for the young and the old alike? We go forward in hope.

ACKNOWLEDGEMENTS

There must be few authors who do not owe a great debt of gratitude to many people, and there is a temptation to allow this to become a very long section, which I will aim to keep brief. I wish to thank the community projects, care homes and care groups that have supported this book from the outset by welcoming me to visit and talk at length, and the older people and carers who have shared their thoughts. In particular but not exclusively: the Abbeyfield Society, Anchor Hanover, Cambridgeshire County Council and its Neighbourhood Cares team, Glenfields, Hallmark Care Homes (in particular for also enabling the lengthy and essential transcriptions), Milford Care Homes, Nightingale Hammerson, Well-being Teams and Wren Hall.

Baroness Sally Greengross, Lorraine Morley (author of one of the chapters), Marian Barnes, Elizabeth Baxter of Holy Rood House, Stephen Burke of United for All Ages and April Dobson of Hallmark have all been wonderful in sharing contacts and introductions and encouraging my efforts.

Claire Jarvis and Catherine Jones of Routledge could not have been more helpful and patient in guiding me through the publishing process – thank you.

On a personal level, so many thanks: to my husband, Trevor, for supporting me throughout the entire process (and for many cups of coffee); to Lesley Turney for the careful transcriptions; to Joanne Parker for advice, proofing and critical reading; to Wendy Rainbow for unfailing faith that I would complete the book. And finally to Joy, the Labradoodle puppy who joined our household just as this book was reaching fruition, for her grounding presence. She is now planning her career as a therapy dog.

1

RELATIONAL CARE

Improving lives for older people, carers and families

Introduction: challenge and change

Older people are ourselves: they are us as we are now, or will be in the future. They are human beings, each unique in their needs, fears and desires, and each one part of the human family, with its collective needs, fears and desires. Older people are not a commodity or a problem or a challenge. The challenge for society is to think and act in different ways that allow everyone to be retained within the human family and enable each individual to live the best life possible within the constraints of ageing.

Is meeting this challenge possible in financial, political and practical terms? That is the question this book explores and starts to answer from lived experience and the results of pioneering work.

One immediate answer would be to pose a counter question: in ethical and moral terms, can society afford to ignore this challenge? While this is a very valid question, it would be naïve to suggest it can be a full response. All social changes come with a price tag: for individuals, families and communities. So to look at it another way: is it more expensive in economic and ethical terms to ensure that older people are cared about, cared for and have the freedom to give care to others, or is it ultimately more expensive to problematise or commoditise them?

My aim is to address this basic question – which is in itself both profoundly rooted in morality and yet at the same time very practical in its implications – by looking at how we can create environments that enable individuality, encourage relationships and nurture human flourishing.

Much has been written about the philosophy of ageing and the deepest questions that we all face as we get older. And more is starting to be written about the practicalities of how we can live our daily lives as we age. Answers to some of the most profound questions find their expression in the everyday environment in which we function and thrive (or not). This book is intended to illustrate how a positive philosophical approach is enabled by and expressed through the apparently mundane, something as simple as the positioning of seating in a lounge. It really is possible for carers and those cared for to achieve more control over the details of their daily life, opening the way for greater contentment and fulfilment.

In *Developing a Relational Model of Care for Older People (2018)*, my co-author and I proposed that 'relational care' (a term explored later in this chapter) facilitates the wellbeing of older people, those who care for them and their families. Based on extensive interviews and analysis, we described how this approach manifests itself in everyday life and the types of benefits it offers. In this context, we have since been asked by care providers, older people and their relatives: 'But what works? How do we do it?'. This book will offer ideas for models that enable the most beneficial types of relational care, and it will do so very much through the voices of others, exploring their experiences and how they feel about their lives.

Transformation and flourishing

Care cannot only be given; it must also be received and returned. The concept of care ethics, discussed later in this chapter, prioritises 'relationships and responsibilities', as opposed to the 'rights and rules' emphasised by justice ethics, and thereby redirects thinking and practice towards a whole environment of interconnectivity.

The vital importance of relationships is now widely accepted as transformative to the lives of all involved in the care of older people, yet favouring the conditions for them to get established has a long way to go, in policy, planning and practice. Perhaps this is in part because we are uncertain about what 'transformation' means or looks like, and it is only by seeing it in action and listening to voices describe it that it gains power and becomes worthy of pursuit.

It is about profound change, being able to live life more fully, to feel oneself a person who is respected and loved as an individual, to have a sense of security, of being known and knowing others. It has been called 'an inner awakening' (Jewell, 2004, p. 133).

Transforming people's lives requires transformative practice: ways of being together that 'allow us to imagine ourselves differently [through] a process of projection that takes place through relationships with others and with cultural images and representations' (Barnes et al., 2018, p. 160). It is not mainly about (although may include) changes in health status and medication but about being in a situation where people can re-discover themselves: 'counter to a popular belief in decline and loss of capacity and relevance, older people contain within themselves the potential of greater personal resources' (Jewell, 2004, p. 150). By focussing on avoiding 'decrepitude', 'we blind ourselves to the opportunities that exist to change individual experience of ageing for the better' (Gawande, p. 35). Mowat and Mowat allude to the 'social assumptions' about old age bringing decline, diminishment and fragility as 'pernicious and powerful' (2018, p. 122) because they carry elements of truth but are not the truth.

This book is based on listening to the experiences of all types of people involved in older care, to help understand how it feels when things are done differently. Below are some of the things that interviewees have said to me about the experience of finding and observing real change once they are in the right environment, sometimes brought about by simple alterations in life, sometimes by a profound reconfiguring of comprehension: the environmental factors that enable the criteria for relational care and life change are the subject of this book.

CHANGING LIVES

'Some people go from just wanting to be served to being the life of the party' (care home owner).

'If someone has been living on their own without much conversation, naturally they become a bit withdrawn; we support them gently to find their natural path to getting used to company' (manager).

'Would you say life is much different since moving here?' 'Much, much better' (resident).

'Moving from living independently in your own home to needing 24-hour care [is completely different] so the team help them build those new, unique relationships' (manager).

'Her daughter spoke to me saying she can't believe the change in her mum since being here. She's so much happier, joining in, more talkative. A different person' (residential care worker).

'If there were more holistic care in hospital, people would be more likely to thrive and may not need to go into a residential home' (community project team member).

'They do settle in and relax; it's very daunting when they first come in' (residential care worker).

'I was clinically depressed when I came here. It's helped me get my life back; I love it' (activities co-ordinator).

'Coming into a care home isn't the end of exploration and adventure; in fact it can be the start' (director).

'This has opened her up as a person' (project manager).

'It shouldn't be a negative, but seen as a move to somewhere where people will take away some of your worries and you can have a great time!' (carer).

'If someone goes from hospital to a care home, the transition is much better if our team is involved' (community project team member).

'I want to make a success of the move here; I've thought it through and already had three visits, before I had to come here from hospital' (resident).

Transformation in later years from a retreat into loneliness, lack of capability, loss of interest in self and others and towards positive engagement, even if limited by physical or cognitive constraints, argues for 'flourishing', for being nurtured to grow and thrive. Is 'flourishing' akin to 'wellbeing'? The latter is often used in talking about old age, as a state to be created and measured; physical, mental and spiritual wellbeing are all frequently under consideration.

The environment that nurtures positive engagement is one where everyone who is interacting, older people, carers, volunteers and families, can thrive and not feel diminished or dismissed by society. 'In order to flourish…. I have to have good relations with others, and people cannot flourish at times of war, strife and dissent' (King in Jewell, 2004, p. 134).

What such an environment might look like, the models on which it might be based and the varied ways of achieving it are explored in future chapters.

FLOURISHING IS ABOUT GETTING THE MOST OUT OF LIFE AS IT IS

'We have a lot of good days and only a few bad ones' (residential care worker).

You still have opportunities to learn and to discover and to give to the community' (client of community project).

'I was amazed at what that [resident with dementia] could read, so now we've developed a reading assessment and started a book club' (manager).

'There's always been staff that bring their children in, and the older people light up when they're around' (owner).

'We've been out and about together to other care homes and a cake competition'. 'I really enjoyed it' (carer/resident).

Wellbeing

According to the *Oxford English Dictionary*, 'wellbeing' means 'the state of being comfortable, healthy or happy', while the *Cambridge English Dictionary* uses the equally acceptable hyphenated form and defines well-being as 'the state of being healthy and happy'. However, its widespread use in the worlds of health and social care encompasses a number of notions, some quite vague; citing David Seedhouse (Mohan in Jewell, p. 170), wellbeing is 'irreducibly subjective, and the meaning and content of the term …fluctuate, depending on who is using it and why it is being used'. These elements of subjectivity and variation are worth bearing in mind, especially when it comes to measurement (a contested area which is discussed in Appendix A), but it remains a useful word, and one that is used so generally that it cannot be avoided.

Barnes et al. (2018) explore the concept of wellbeing as a 'process' rather than a 'state' (p. 125), as 'subjective' (p. 128) and as both a personal and a social phenomenon linked to one another, as the individual will inevitably be affected by the general. 'To develop an understanding of what wellbeing means that is useful.… Requires a more grounded and contextualised way of approaching how people make sense of what is happening in their lives and what it is they value' (ibid., p. 130). In fact – there should be more listening!

Importantly, Barnes et al. observe – as I too have found in numerous interviews – that talking to older people reveals there is not a direct link between health and wellbeing: 'some of our interviewees were adamant that health problems and physical limitations associated with these did not automatically mean low wellbeing [although they] necessitated adaptions' (ibid., p. 133). And most significantly they continue: 'we have started to identify what is probably *the most significant factor impacting wellbeing: the nature of the relationships they have with other people*' (ibid., my italics, p. 99).

As to whether wellbeing and flourishing are interchangeable, I would argue that the latter suggests a more active sense of personal growth and human potential being fulfilled – encompassing creativity, joy, love and hope – so would use it to describe very positive states and situations in which people are able to be 'the best they can be'. To me, this also requires a recognition of spirituality in its widest form, although acknowledging that not everyone would be comfortable with this concept, which is discussed later in this chapter.

Listening to voices

The phrase 'Nothing about me without me' came to prominence in the disability rights movement of the 1990s, having originated in medieval central Europe. It was adopted by the NHS (National Health Service) in the form 'No decision about me without me' and is now accepted as the desirable way of planning individual treatment and group services. Yet every day, care is provided to older people in a variety of ways and settings, without consulting them or listening to who they are and what matters to them. There are so many 'valid' reasons for this, such as lack of time, shortage of carers, assumptions based on received learning, perceived incapacity of some older people to express their wishes, misunderstandings in communication, the reticence of many care recipients to speak up and the belief that their (younger) family knows best. The list is endless.

Many of the supposedly valid reasons cited above can be overcome, but reform is only possible if we actually listen attentively to older people, their friends and relatives with a genuine desire to learn and, as I found, go beyond listening: 'Spending time in homes with older people as part of a research project is not just about listening; it is about absorbing, and being absorbed… travelling beyond observation into feeling' (Woodward and Kartupelis, 2018, p. 49). Similarly, there is a need to listen carefully to carers. While good, involved managers and directors of organisations offer valuable knowledge that must be heeded, those who are part of the day-to-day life of a care environment are the ones who can share unique insight and understanding.

There is also a pressing need to shift thinking away from negatives such as the fear of dependence on the part of older people, their accustomed state being one of decrepitude and their seat being 'in St Peter's waiting room', the idea that after a certain age, people only look backwards: 'implicit in most perspectives on ageing and gerontology is the assumption that, whatever a senior's health status, he or she has no sense of a future, no anticipation of new experiences or the joyous potential of tomorrow' (Koch, 2000, p. 14). The voices of older people talking about planned outings, lively friendships, new hobbies even in the fourth age and forthcoming family celebrations tell us something very different.

Likewise there should be a move away from negatives about the care sector, such as the belief that giving care is a one-way, low-skilled, high-turnover job that can be performed by anyone without much training or support; that putting public funding into the sector 'robs' younger people; that grim environments will not be a source of complaint and that high expectations are only on the part of relatives rather than the older people themselves; and that 'love' is an unsuitable or unprofessional word in the context of care. While this book focusses on positives, there are some implied warnings about what can happen in the worst settings in the chapters that follow.

The value of listening can easily be underestimated, both in terms of planning for the future and learning from the past, and can be unintentionally disregarded: 'The elderly are silent speakers whose complex perspective is lost to us in the advancing, busy present', warns Koch (ibid., p. 3). Their input is often lacking in the studies intended to shape their lives: 'one of the weaknesses of much of the gerontological research …. [l]ies in the absence of input from older people' (Woodward, 2008, p. 201). Barnes et al. addressed this issue in their study described in *Re-imagining Old Age* (2018) through using participatory research, not only taking the testimony of older people but working with a team of interviewers whose ages ranged from the 60s to over 90,

> reject[ing] the assumption that scientific method will generate objective and rational knowledge without any recognition or acknowledgement of whose knowledge or voices are represented in the process, nor how power itself frames the ways in which research questions are conceptualised.
>
> *(Ibid., p. 66)*

In the context of research and evaluation in the healthcare system, the viewpoints usually sought are those of national organisations and the professional staff in provider bodies. There is insufficient call for 'A third viewpoint …. of the individual persons who receive the care. This viewpoint might seem appropriate and desirable but is seldom used' (Cluff and Binstock, 2001, p. 206). This observation is at least equally valid in the context of social care. It is the vital 'experiential knowledge' that differs from other types of knowledge and 'offers an often practical or pragmatic insight into "what works" from the perspective of those directly affected as well as encompassing an insight into what is valued' (Barnes et al., 2018, p. 45).

Developing a Relational Model of Care for Older People (2018) was based on over 100 interviews with residents, carers, managers and volunteers in Abbeyfield homes and sheltered housing. It not only reflected those voices but also encouraged them to guide the study by generating themes to explore, using the learning from them to propose an approach to residential living based on what appeared to most matter in that particular setting and would nurture positive interdependence. However, there is equally a real interest in how to create and manage other types of setting to achieve flourishing relationships and better outcomes. This book draws on 50 new interviews in 13 different settings, using the same semi-structured, exploratory approach to present a picture of the possible through the words of people who are already living that possible: 'We need relationships on the basis of which we can grow, learn and experience wellbeing' (Barnes et al., 2018, p. 26).

What can go right: successful models and innovation

Setting aside for now the challenge of defining wellbeing, there is a broad consensus that sound interpersonal (and indeed interspecies!) relationships are the foundation for contentment and for flourishing at all ages. Examples of this consensus, how it has grown and how it is expressed underlie all the models and ideas in this book. Each of the models and innovations have been chosen to represent a care environment at its best, whether it be a community project or a residential arrangement. Each will be presented with a short history and description and then explored through the questions: What does this look like in practice? What does this feel like for the people involved? What practical lessons can be learnt from it? The answers to these critical questions indicate how the model might be used or adapted by practitioners, and to what type of older people it might be most appealing or suitable. The purpose of this book is to review and present good practice and innovation in creating care environments that work for all involved in them and learning points. The intention is not to review and compare good and bad practice but to focus on the best that can be achieved and how to make it happen.

Most babies born in Western countries in 2000 will live to celebrate their 100th birthdays (*The Lancet*, 2009, cited in Storlie, 2015, p. 176). Statistics from the ONS (August 2018) indicate the projected growth of the ageing population. In 2016 there were 11.8 million UK residents aged 65 and over (18% of the population), and by 2066 this is projected to be 20.4 million (26% of the population). In 2016 there were 1.6 million people aged 85 and over (2% of the population), and this is projected to be 3.2 million (4% of the population) by mid-2041 and 5.1 million (7% of the population) by 2066. By 2050 one in four people will be aged 65 and over. Of the current 11.8 million people over 65, 5.4 million people are aged 75 plus, 1.6 million are aged 85 plus, 579,776 are 90 plus and 14,430 are centenarians. As the population continues to age, demand for care will increase and the types of care needed will change.

This information will therefore be widely relevant: to older people considering their future care; to their friends and families helping them navigate the possibilities; to those working in the care sector or training to do so as they decide where they wish to be placed to give of their best and to be respected and supported; to managers of projects and care homes who are assessing or developing them; to directors in the public, private and third sectors who are making decisions about care delivery and resource allocation; and to those who influence policy and wish to plan for the future on the basis of what works and what matters to people.

How the nature of caring for older people has developed

The roots of where we are now

The recent history of older adult care in the Western world affects so much current practice: our fears, our hopes, what we assume about the progression of life and what we expect to hear when we talk to older people and carers. There is a danger of perpetuating all sorts of ideas that hold back the best in favour of the mediocre and established, and it is therefore well worth looking at how our current system has developed and how the underlying thinking has evolved.

Referring to a conversation with Keren Wilson, the US pioneer of assisted living, Gawande asks: 'how [can] ordinary people age without having to choose between neglect and institutionalization? It remains amongst the most uncomfortable questions we face' (Gawande, 2014, p. 103). That is the question this book will help to answer, by looking afresh at what constitutes an institution. As Gawande asks about the innovative US project Chase Memorial Nursing Home, transformed by Bill Thomas in the early 1990s driven by the concept of the 'thriving abundance of life' rather than' despair in every room' (ibid., p. 115): 'Were they running an institution or providing a home?' (ibid., p. 122).

Until the nineteenth century, as people grew older and more infirm, they were expected to live with younger family members and be supported by them, and unless they had sufficient wealth, they had little alternative. There were alms houses, and some hospital care provided mainly by Christian charities, but no state aid, no old age pension and of course no NHS. The Victorian Poor Laws led to the creation of workhouses, largely dreaded for their draconian regimes, stigma and separation of families. In the United States the equivalent was the poorhouses, and Gawande notes: 'nothing provoked greater terror for the aged than the prospect of such institutions. Nonetheless, by the 1920s and 1930s.... two thirds of poorhouse residents were elderly' (ibid., 2014, p. 63). Workhouses in Britain were not intended primarily for older people, but these were the institutions where they ended up in the worst-case scenario, and it is a revelation the extent to which they still cast a shadow.

In the first half of the twentieth century, 'institutional care' designed specifically for older people started to be developed, and the UK system became distinguished by the differentiation of healthcare provision defined by the NHS Act of 1946 and 'social care' for the 'frail and old' under the National Assistance Act of 1948. Healthcare was supplied by the NHS and free at the point of access, while social care provision fell mainly to Local Authorities and in part (as ever) to charities. (In the United States, 'nursing homes' have a different history, having been set up to 'clear out hospital beds' (Gawande, 2014, p. 71).)

In the 1980s, changes to funding enabled independent providers to move in and create a market, regulated by the state under the Registered Homes Act of 1984. Homes could be registered to provide residential care, nursing care or both; under the more recent Care Standards Act (2000), the distinction is now called 'personal' or 'nursing' care. Ownership has moved substantially towards the independent sector following funding changes in the 1980s and very few homes are now owned by Local Authorities. In 2017, there were around 5,500 different providers in the UK operating 11,300 care homes for the older adults, but only 5% of beds were directly provided by Local Authorities, the remaining 95% by the independent sector (both for-profit and charitable providers) (https://www.gov.uk/government/publications/care-homes-market-study).

However, community-based provision of social and personal care remains under the aegis (directly or indirectly) of local government, and examples are discussed later, such as the very successful Neighbourhood Cares scheme in Cambridgeshire.

The history of providing care for those who are frail or ageing has tended to lead increasingly to a private market economy (and a very substantial one), which, for reasons that will be considered subsequently, are not necessarily conducive to good relational care. Its ultimate aims are not always the wellbeing of older people or their carers, although these factors may be important to its operational model, and this tension is addressed in Chapter 6. The question is: are our priorities to keep older people out of harm's way and largely out of mainstream society, or to enable them to find meaning in later life and to enjoy the 'abundance' that people of other ages rightly expect? Describing the 'Eden Alternative' – referred to in Chapter 3 – Lynne Hugo writes of a place where older people currently incarcerated in the care home she is visiting, Golden View, could instead be themselves, playing with animals, helping children learn to read and 'would be needed again'.

> When I think of a … home where there are quiet areas for visiting, reading… where my hair colour is my own business…where community is actively built; where gardens flourish indoors and outdoors along with animals and birds, I feel hope. That is nothing short of miraculous when I compare it to life at Golden View.
>
> *(2005, p. 76)*

In this 'battle over fundamentally different worldviews' (Gawande, 2014, p. 122), amplifying the voices of those who live within the outcomes surely advocates for a worldview based not on divisions and fractures between wealth, generations or political ideology but on love, compassion and flourishing.

Attitudes, policy and current practice

The context of ageing is changing, but responses to older age have not yet caught up. 'Our grandparents' ageing was mediated and influenced by an assumption of decline and forgetfulness… and by strong village-community lives…and by duty to be done' (Mowat and Mowat 2018, p. 101). Hence

> one of the paradoxes in the UK [is that] policies firmly state that people should want to remain in their own homes and with their families… at the same time as our family structures and relationships are undergoing major change.
>
> *(Ibid., p. 105)*

In fact, 'just 10 percent of Europeans over age 85 live with their children' (Gawande, 2014, p. 21).

The Victorian Poor Law cited above presents

> the challenge to leave behind [its] legacy… that appears in those of our current policies which are still focussed on determining who is *not* entitled to assistance; on a continuing dependence on segregation in care homes which for many still have reminders of the workhouse; and on continued territorial differences between local authorities.
>
> *(Woodward, 2008, p. 187)*

> Until the 1960s, ageing was largely understood as a period of inevitable decline towards death…. A contraction of contact. This was challenged by the emergence of 'activity theory' … the core [of which] is that continued social participation can contribute to longer and better quality later life.
>
> *(Barnes et al., 2018, p. 16)*

However, this new paradigm was predicated on the assumption that older people had previously followed a pattern of dropping out of society and that 'active' (or 'healthy' or 'successful' or 'productive') ageing would enable individuals to take more responsibility for themselves with health-promoting behaviour and social engagement. While this idea has the merit of encouraging social relationships, it also has the potential to diminish the older person, for 'personal growth, even if one is frail and dependent, [to be] neither noticed nor valued' (Holstein, 2015, p. 105).

The move away from institutional or dependent care to viewing self-responsibility and articulation as the preferred norm was marked by the 1990 National Health Service and Community Care Act. Sadly, this did not bring the two services together in any appreciable way, nor, although intended to empower older people to be more involved in decisions about their own care, did it 'create any formal rights to participate in specific governance mechanisms' (Barnes et al., 2018, p. 48) in spite of a plethora of initiatives, such as the Better Government for Older People programme, as they all fell by the wayside. The UK Advisory Forum on Ageing was set up in 2010 but closed down again in 2015, 'leaving no specific mechanisms through which older people's voices were to be heard within the government' (ibid., p. 52).

Fluctuations in policy and the continuing growth of the 'market' have led to a considerable range of care delivery mechanisms and a greater variety of institutions, public and private, formal and informal. These include community-based social and cross-disciplinary teams, day centres, assisted living, sheltered housing, co-housing, self-organised and self-owned communities, personal and nursing care homes and variations on these themes. Overseas models have been adopted in the UK and vice versa, with varying success. Many of these models will be considered in this book, in terms of the ways in which they can create the conditions for relational care.

Not only has policy been affected by the legacy of history but also by the hegemony of medicalisation: the belief that everything can be cured by drugs or surgery, and if it cannot, then the only other option is despair or decline.

> The relatively marginalised position that older people occupy in modern day health and social care systems is best understood in the context of geriatric medicine and, in particular, the influence that the 'medical model' of care has exerted on our views of what constitutes successful treatment .... which [has] implicitly reinforced a 'cure' based health care system...... Interestingly, ageist attitudes were evident from the inception of the NHS, with the Beveridge Report warning about the resource implications of being 'lavish to old age'.
>
> *(Nolan et al., 2006, p. 15)*

Had this predominance of trust in health interventions for older people resulted in joined-up thinking and working between health and social care, it could have been very positive, but on the contrary, it has created a division between the two disciplines, the problems of which – including unequal funding and ageism – are explored in Chapter 6.

At this point it is worth acknowledging that social care is still seen as the poor relation of the NHS, because this fact underlies the perceived greater reluctance to spend on the former, and the ills that arise from this in terms of providing optimum environments for relational care. Again, it is a question of worldviews. Is the UK economy – the sixth largest in the world – to be the servant or the master of its population?

Person-centred care

The concept of person-centred care was perhaps intended to be, at least in part, an answer to the question of who controls the wellbeing of older people in need of any type of care: themselves or a 'one size fits all' system? 'Themselves' would seem to be the enlightened response, and in 2001, 'The National Service Framework (NSF) for Older People' (DoH, 2001) was announced, which for the first time set national standards of care for older people in England. Two closely linked principles lie at the heart of the NSF: 'the promotion of person-centred care, and the rooting out of age discrimination in the NHS' (Nolan et al., 2006, p. 17).

There are a number of ways of looking at person-centred care. It can be about the choice to purchase what one believes one needs and make decisions about how to spend a care budget provided by state funding (and of course topped up by private money if it is available). It can also be about shifting the focus of care away from what best serves the providing organisation or system towards what best serves the recipient individual. The former can lead to unintended consequences, as we will see later in this chapter; the latter is a worthy aim but has led to assumptions about interaction that hold back a better way of caring.

Defining 'person-centred' is not straightforward: 'Person-centred care is an often quoted but ill-defined concept that has nevertheless exerted a considerable influence on policy, practice and academic literatures' (ibid., p. 114). Writing in *My Home Life*, Bridges says: 'There are still theoretical concerns about what is meant by person-centred and personhood (the central attribute of being a person)' (2007, p. 52), but in the context of dementia care, she proposes Brooker's (2004) four elements of: treating people as individuals, valuing them, looking at the world from their perspective and providing a positive social environment.

Storlie describes person-centred service as 'a philosophy that views the older adult as a person first and as a patient, client, customer or facility resident second.... It places the older person at the heart of any decision that would impact him or her' (2015, p. 38). Although 'no universally accepted definitions of person-centred care yet exist, there are widely agreed upon objectives' (ibid., p. 39), which include recognising individuality and autonomy, having supportive staff and establishing a 'partnership' that enables the older adult to contribute to resolving their own concerns.

The concept of person-centred care is based on psycho-social theories, which can be explored particularly through the work of the psychologists Erik Erikson (1902–1994) and Carl Rogers (1902–1987), who pioneered client-centred therapy in the 1940s and 1950s. Storlie traces these developments in *Person-Centred Communication with Older Adults* (2015), taking his examples primarily from many interactions that are likely to be transient in their nature (ibid., p. 5). He looks particularly at establishing 'rapport' in communication, and it is worth noting that rapport is about feeling 'seen, heard and understood' (ibid., p. 47) and about '*mutual* understanding and acceptance' (ibid., p. 41, my italics).

More recently, the move towards 'personalisation' has become one practical expression of person-centred philosophy: a programme whereby 'users' of social care services who qualified for state support have been allocated 'cash for care' budgets to choose and pay for their own services. While this can suit some younger people, it has also further stimulated the creation of a 'market' discussed in the final chapter, which does not necessarily favour older care recipients, depending on what is available, how it is priced, to what extent its beneficiaries have had any input into its creation and what skills it requires to manage the funding at an individual level. 'Consumerism' has negatives as well as positives for the consumer.

In considering the person-centred approach as a positive step towards relational care, it is useful to remember how the worst type of care – the workhouse, the nursing homes set up to clear hospital wards, the dreaded institutions – treated individuals as objects, burdens and commodities (and some still do). There have always been staff who have worked against inhumane systems, but the move towards person-centred philosophy validated and supported them.

> A person-centred approach is not just the individual practitioner's responsibility but a philosophy for the whole organisation… managers and staff [must] be adequately supported in developing person-centred approaches to care. [This] can also provoke anxiety and discomfort as staff come to terms with the emotional nature of their work.
>
> *(ibid., p. 63)*

In other words, to be 'person-centred' ought to require forming sound relationships between individuals – but in practice it may not.

Advantages and challenges of person-centred care

In medical care, the Hippocratic Oath presupposes the centrality of the patient and the benevolence of the practitioner. However, advances in medicine have brought an increasing focus on 'remaining alive [being] the ultimate good' (Cassell in Cluff and Binstock, 2001, p. 110), a focus which can then lead to patients being viewed as a collection of organs to be cured or problems to be solved. Such objectification can creep into 'patient-centred social care' if organisations are not alert to the possibility.

It is notable that Storlie's definition given above does not mention amongst the objectives of the person-centred model, the possibility of the older adult contributing to anything other than their own wellbeing, which implies no recognition of, and hence focus on, their contribution to others or their community. Recognising individuality is important, and entails moving away from 'the idea of homogenous groups of "older people" who can be categorised, stereotyped' (Mowat and Mowat, 2018, p. 69) but most individual lives are expressed through 'relationships that are mutual…and interdependent' (ibid., p. 71).

Person-centred practice has also led to an emphasis on 'understanding' older people through their biographies and stories. Truly listening, hearing and responding is a wonderful gift but demands that carers reciprocate and give something of themselves in return, or it can be an empty exercise of recording as a 'task'. There is also a danger of stereotyping older people as having an interest only in the past, with no expectations of the future, although ensuring that there are mechanisms to share memories with younger people through school visits or museum projects can partially resolve this challenge.

The motivation of improved communication can only be welcome and is likely to address the curse of 'elderspeak', which is 'the polar opposite of the person-centred approach' and is 'dehumanising and objectifying' (ibid., p. 80). While this is true, and care should by no means be centred on the needs of the provider as an organisation, shifting all the focus onto the older person and away from the carers can inadvertently lead to unwanted consequences. One is the risk of disempowering elders by not acknowledging their wider social value or contribution and very frail older people becoming 'vulnerable to being treated like children, in need of what services call "all care"' (Mowat and Mowat, 2018, p. 142). While this is certainly not the intention of person-centred philosophy – indeed arguably the opposite – the humanity, value and individuality of the person can be lost as they become the object of care unless they remain engaged with the community they occupy.

Disempowerment of the care recipient, however well meant the services lavished on them, can also have the effect of adding to the stress of the carer, who may feel they can never do enough. This can be the case where family care is being provided to an older relative, especially if all the onus falls on a small group of immediate family. Mowat and Mowat describe a family who felt they must conform to certain expectations as their father aged: he must be 'looked after... they would phone regularly, visit and fuss around his kitchen, tutting about the lack of edible food... they created a mutually reassuring dependency' (ibid., p. 89) (the shackles of which he later threw off!).

There are also negatives of 'over-care' in residential settings, where paid carers can feel continually harassed. As we will see, a shift towards relational care can, if handled carefully, reduce staff and management stress by creating a more supportive work environment. Discussing workplace stress, Storlie – as many advisors and supervisors would – recommends setting 'professional boundaries' (2015, p. 122), yet later says: 'When a provider genuinely experiences positive feelings such as appreciation, compassion *and love*, his or her autonomic nervous system responds favourably and brain function is enhanced' (ibid., p. 149, my italics). So, positive feelings and feedback enhance wellbeing. Getting that balance right in terms of carer wellbeing is part of good relational care.

This observation reflects Dodson and Zincavage's summary of their review of employment in US care homes in 'It's Like a Family': 'We argue that meeting a growing public need for long-term care demands an ethic of reciprocity: considerate, high-quality care for those who need it, and respect and decent compensation for those who provide this critical labour' (2007, p. 907).

Person-centred care in practice

Moving the focus from what is useful to the care providing organisation towards what may be valuable for the older people it is there to help is a critical change in outlook, demanding that the organisation changes its basis of operation and that it helps carers change their perspective to see the world through older eyes (see Crisp, p. 126 on developing this type of empathy) and breaking down barriers to poor communication and understanding.

The US residential homes surveyed by Dodson and Zincavage became more reliant on their care staff as they moved to a more person-centred approach. These were

> the people who possessed a critical understanding of residents' preferences, recognized day-to-day changes in resident status, and thus were the most capable of providing care centred on the individual. Managers referred to CNAs [care staff] as being the 'eyes and ears' of the facility or the 'hearts and hands' of care; the people who really understood the needs and condition of the residents.
>
> *(ibid., p. 914)*

But these demands on carers mean that they need time, support and training, and there was concern that the person-centred care adopted by the interviewees may just be window-dressing: 'Encouraging caregivers to form deep bonds with residents and thus go out of their way to take good care of them was discussed as humane *as well as a boon to the institutional bottom line*' (ibid., p. 915, my italics).

Once person-centred care is fully practiced, that is, when people cease to be seen as objects, it starts to morph into relational care, because everyone involved has *de facto* become recognised as a unique individual. The Butterfly Model developed for dementia care homes by David Sheard et al., mentioned later in this chapter and elsewhere, exemplifies this progress of a sensitive, person-centred model into relational care.

What is relational care?

Definitions and usage

> The task of washing a patient in the evening after tea can be achieved very economically....But the minute it takes at the end to squeeze her hand, or give her a goodnight kiss on the forehead, or just stop and look into her eyes and say what a wonderful person she is…is transformative.
>
> *(Wilcock in Jewell, 2004, p. 65)*

Considering the philosophy of person-centred care, how it has developed and the various ways it is expressed in practice, has led to the conclusion that relationships of all types (families, friends, carers) are critical to wellbeing and flourishing and that care provided to older people should be centred on promoting relationships rather than solely on the individual.

This recognition of relationships as central to care is becoming the focus of increased interest and research but is a relatively recent area of investigation, and the terminology is still somewhat fluid as to how the phenomenon should be distinguished from 'person-centred care'. Some, including the author, have used the term 'relational' to describe the phenomenon of a network of caring relationships, not centred on any single individual, but encouraging individual wellbeing and resilience. However, the term 'relational care' can also be used to describe care given by or within the family, for example, by Barken & Lowndes, 'Supporting family involvement in long-term residential care: Promising practices for relational care', *Qualitative Health Research* (2018).

'Relationship-centred' is used as a descriptor in the non-family sense by Nolan (2008), summarised in the one-pager 'Moving from person-centred care to relationship-centred care', published online by Partnerships in Dementia Care.

Jasmyne Rockwell in 'From personal-centred to relational care: Expanding the focus in residential care facilities' in *Journal of Gerontological Social Work* (2012) – the observations of which very much chime with my work – uses 'relational' to mean almost exactly the concept I describe in *Developing a Relational Model of Care* (Woodward and Kartupelis, 2018): 'multidirectional relationships ... fostering meaningful engagement for residents and staff' (p. 234), and she goes on to explore 'the therapeutic potential of relationships and relational care'. Rockwell's article is based on a qualitative study of four social workers and one physician, undertaken in Canada.

The Butterfly Model, developed by David Sheard as a culture change programme for dementia care homes (Dementia Care Matters, 2013), is interesting in this context because although it takes as its starting point person-centred care, it actually focusses on feelings and 'being' rather than 'doing' and talks about 'relationship focused support' (ibid., p. 2) rather than about individuals. As we will see in Chapter 3, adopting this model leads to a care home embedding the very features that nurture relational care.

Barnes et al. talk of a 'relational approach to wellbeing' as 'understanding how everyday interactions with people, places, services and cultural representations impact on people's sense of their own worth and their capacity to contribute as well as receive' (2018, p. 131), and this book considers in particular how the first of these – relationships between people – is affected by the last three – places, services and cultural representations.

So to conclude: a decision about terminology has to be made, and in this book, the term 'relational care' is the descriptor that will be used rather than 'relationship-centred care'.

Key criteria that support the benefits of relational care are: respect, generating self-worth and dignity; providing a feeling of knowing others and being known and accepted by them; enabling safety and security; and most importantly fostering reciprocity – 'interactions and relationships in which [people are] able to contribute something to others' (ibid., p. 134). These are the basis of living that help people to discern meaning in life and become more resilient, and most importantly that can be supported by the right environmental factors. The following chapters are about creating that environment.

Meaning and purpose in life

The value of relational care is predicated on a number of assumptions about what matters to people, regardless of age. These include the assumptions that most people feel greater contentment and fulfilment (which are commonly used to describe 'wellbeing') if they are not lonely, if they interact with others, if they feel known and accepted, if they believe they have meaning in life and if they can build resilience. 'Loneliness' is discussed in more detail in the next chapter, in relation to its prevalence and different types of community-based care. It is worth briefly looking here at the ideas of 'meaning in life' and 'resilience'.

Is it possible to identify what 'meaning in life' encompasses in everyday conversation and thinking, is it a 'real' (achievable) ambition and why does it matter so much? For the purposes of the relational care context, we will assume it is 'real' insofar as it is a factor mentioned by real people as mattering to them, and therefore it must matter in creating environments of flourishing. The concept has been explored and dissected by many psychotherapists and psychologists, to say nothing of poets and novelists and philosophers, in many millions of words, so it would be easy to get diverted into a very long disquisition on the subject – much longer than this book!

Humans are programmed to look for meanings in everything, however random. As we sit in a waiting room, for example, we often see 'faces' or animal shapes in abstract wallpaper patterns. The Rorschach ink tests, whereby subjects are asked to interpret a completely random smudge of ink to give insight into their state of mind, are based on the same principle. The early-twentieth-century Gestalt theory in philosophy and psychology (gestalt is German for 'form' or 'configuration') proposes practice based on these ideas of pattern and connectedness: that there is a wholeness we seek in interpreting life experiences, which argues for integration of body, mind and spirit. As life progresses, the urge to feel that there is some pattern in life, that one's time has had some purpose, and still does, is generally important to a sense of self-identity and emotional wellbeing.

Cultural background will affect how this urge to make sense of occurrences and surroundings expresses itself in practice and creating self-identity within the wider community – for example a deeply held faith will influence views of life meaning, and Western society is more inclined towards seeking meaning from achievements (doing) than from life's journey (being), which influences Eastern philosophy. 'Our cultures, and the view of the world they represent, are important.... They provide a sense of meaning and help us maintain the belief that our lives are significant' (Crisp, 2015, p. 11).

'Meaning in life' is generally accepted as relevant to contentment in older age; for example, in *My Home Life* (2007), Bridges advocates preserving a sense of self (and hence a better quality of life) through a 'personally meaningful environment', 'meaningful objects' and 'meaningful activities' (p. 51 onwards). Meaning and purpose also encompass an element of affirmation about oneself as being needed and part of society: 'older people.... can feel that life no longer has point or purpose ...that they are not important to anyone anymore' (Jewell, 2004, p. 20).

Importantly for the concept of relational care, a recent literature review of the papers about meaning in life for older people found that 'The main source of meaning in life of older persons is human relationships' (Hupkens et al., 2016, abstract). 'For many older people in my studies, the answer to what brings greatest meaning for them has been through relationship with others' (MacKinlay, in ibid., p. 76).

Referring to Josiah Royce's writing on the philosophy of 'loyalty', as in the sense of adherence to a cause, a principle or something closer to home and smaller such as a building project or a pet, Gawande believes we all have a strong need to see ourselves as 'part of something greater: a family, a community or a society... psychologists have used the term "transcendence" for a version of this idea... we have a deep need to identify purposes outside ourselves that make living feel meaningful and worthwhile' (Gawande, 2014, p. 127).

MacKinlay, Jewell, Mowat, Woodward and others have all advocated for forms of relational care within the wider concept and terminology of spiritual life, seeing this as inextricably linked to meaning in life. It is a concept with which not everyone is comfortable, if they do not adhere to any religion or faith or have any belief in an afterlife. Yet viewing spirituality as synonymous with religion is 'to exclude a multitude of people, atheist, agnostic, humanist who may not share such beliefs but have a spirituality that is real' (McSherry, 2006 cited by Woodward, 2008, p. 69).

Setting aside that in any case many people do see themselves as spiritual but not religious, that spirituality is a broader and more universal term than any religion and that not all religious people may embody spiritual values, we need to recognise the importance of spiritual life in the context of relational care, because it may well be important to older people.

The importance of spirituality as we age lies in its disengagement from mental or physical health: it is 'a process of growth that can still flourish when all other growth has stopped and our physical and mental powers begin to decline' because it is 'the most interior dimension of ourselves' (King in Jewell, 2004, p. 127). Woodward calls it 'inner life... character and ethos, ideals and intangible beliefs which hold all together; even values and norms' (2008, p. 67).

It is a truism that we can only respect and love others if we respect and love ourselves and we ourselves have a sense of identity and meaning: 'there is obviously a two-way relationship between carers and cared for, each able to help the other in different ways' (Mowat and Mowat, 2018, p. 40). Environments and interactions that sustain meaning in life are a critical part of relational care.

> **FINDING MEANING**
>
> 'I'm living life as it should be – there isn't another life' (older client).
>
> 'A couple of residents work in the shop; they'll use the till, gives them a sense of purpose' (residential care worker).
>
> 'Residents get purpose from having roles and jobs' (residential care worker).
>
> 'I don't want them to come here to die. I want them to come here to live' (manager).
>
> 'It's about how you help residents fulfil life, be well occupied and achieve' (residential care worker).
>
> 'I have a sense of accomplishment' (project worker).

Resilience

Life always has something new to throw at us, old or young, as Shakespeare's Hamlet recognised when he spoke of the 'slings and arrows of outrageous fortune'. Resilience is about how we cope with life's ups and downs. 'Resilience occurs when an individual experiences stressors and is able to successfully cope with them in a constructive manner. [It] is correlated with improved mental health and lower mortality rates' (Storlie, 2015, p. 113).

Viktor Frankl, imprisoned in a concentration camp, used the phrase 'tragic optimism' to describe being able to experience creativity, love and the belief in something bigger than oneself in the most adverse circumstances, and Mowat and Mowat think 'this morphs into the contemporary idea of the resilient personality' (2018, p. 74). They describe this personality as being 'adaptive', having a sense of 'connectivity' and of 'purpose or meaning' (ibid., p. 65).

Resilience is not just an asset in ageing but is equally important at all ages, and certainly to those giving care, who are reported as finding 'personal growth... and fulfilment' through the caring relationship 'if they themselves are supported and able to keep in good health' (Cluff and Binstock, 2001, p. 67).

Resilience can be built through nurturing the positive emotions that Gawande reports are actually more prevalent in older age as we 'shift towards appreciating everyday pleasures and relationships' (p. 95); through being helped to learn new things (including new technology to keep in touch with family (Barnes et al., 2018, p. 93)); through reconciliation and 'true restitution' with others (Mowat and Mowat, 2018, p. 143); through pondering and sharing life stories that 'help us to reinterpret the past, to help us understand more truly' (ibid., p. 23); and through learning to tolerate uncertainty, that is, 'the part [of life] not yet lived, and the hope inherent in those last times' (MacKinlay in Jewell, 2004, p. 80).

Gawande talks of the courage needed to age: 'Strength in the face of knowledge of what is feared or hoped' (2014, p. 232). This challenge need not be just about accepting loss and sometimes misery but can also be about embracing the new and hopeful and relishing the gifts of 'companionship, everyday routines, good food, the warmth of sunlight on our faces' (ibid., p. 127). Such simple things – yet things that can be denied to older people by their environment.

What distinguishes relational care?

'Love, and feeling loved, is a hardwired prerequisite for managing one's life' (Mowat and Mowat, 2018, p. 30). Resilience, finding meaning in life, building wellbeing and flourishing when physical and cognitive health may no longer be perfect: these things are achieved through 'authentic relationships' (ibid., p. 123) with others and by being part of a wider community.

Reference has already been made to care ethics. There is a considerable amount of literature on this topic, and its history is traced by Gallagher in the original context of nursing practice (Scott, 2017, Chapter 15). He notes: 'There has been scholarship on ethics as applied to care since the 1800s' and by the 1960s there were already 50 published texts on the subject (p. 1). Barnes describes its history in her paper 'Community Care: The Ethics of Care in a Residential Community' (*Ethics and Social Welfare*, 2019), from which these extracts are taken: 'if justice ethics prioritises rights and rules, care ethics emphasises relationships and responsibilities'; 'Care ethicists have undertaken critical policy analysis (Williams 2004) and analysis of policies and practices rarely thought of in this way'; 'Work on care ethics has seen a welcome dialogue between moral philosophers, social scientists and social practitioners (Barnes et al., 2018; Sayer 2011)' (all in ibid., p. 4).

'Care ethics requires a context specific understanding of care as a practice that is attentive to the particularity of relational interdependencies' (ibid., p. 5). At its heart, this approach gives philosophical expression to relational care: 'Care ethics encourages us to recognise that care receiving is as much part of the process of caregiving and that care receivers remain moral agents, even though they may depend on others to ensure basic functioning and survival' (Barnes et al., 2018, p. 29). The study of care ethics continues to evolve, and as Gallagher comments: 'Increasingly there is also a recognition that embracing care does not exclude a commitment to justice and that care needs to be considered in the public as well as in the private domains' (Scott, 2017, Chapter 15, p. 13). Justice and care ethics are not mutually exclusive, and both should inform policy.

There are certainly implications for policy that emerge from studies of ethics, and these are discussed in more detail in Chapter 6. In particular, they highlight the innate contradictions between commonly held opinions (reflected by many popular media): that any failure in care delivery is shameful, yet that tax rises to pay for good care are equally abhorrent; that 'low skilled' migrant labour should be more or less excluded from the UK, yet that public money should not be raised to pay for training and fair payment of home-grown care workers. A balanced media context within which such anomalies could be calmly discussed would be welcome.

An environment that favours the reciprocal practice advocated by care ethics may be based on a philosophical foundation, but achieving it is a very grounded process. To those involved, it is how it feels that matters first, and exploring what enables these feelings will give the answers to the question: What does an environment of flourishing look like?

Systemic relational care and the environmental factors that enable it

'Evidence suggests that it is possible for providers to exert a constructive influence on older adults by thinking, speaking and behaving towards them … in a life affirming manner' (Storlie, 2015, p. 168). 'Understanding an older person's non-physical needs can rarely be done in a short interview ….it is a more radical, longer term commitment to the person in all their mystery and richness' (Woodward, 2008, p. 73).

How do people meeting in, supported by or living in a happy, life-affirming environment describe it? They use a vocabulary that frequently includes 'community', household', 'home' and 'family'. They talk about love, friendship, shared stories and knowledge; the different ways in which they contribute and participate; and how they are being accepted for who they are.

BEING IN A RELATIONAL ENVIRONMENT

'There isn't a staff member who doesn't have a unique relationship with our residents – that includes the catering team and housekeepers' (manager).

'I've always believed in relationship care rather than abstract because they should know me and be able to come to me. The foundation is relationship centred, or how can you give support?' (manager).

'You don't have to have entertainers every day, it can be just a cup of tea with someone you get on with and finding those relationships' (activities manager).

'You can make better decisions based on having a good relationship. You can spot if there's a change of mood' (activities manager).

'Some people take it [i.e., bereavement] harder than others, everybody gets a bond. That's the reason I'm in care, you get those bonds with people. That didn't happen at another home I was in; they were just there for the money, and the care was shocking. I left after three months' (carer).

What are the environmental factors that help people to feel loved, to be themselves and to be able to grow in the ways that they can and wish to? What are the most important criteria supporting relational care? Only once these have been distinguished is it possible to understand how and why some models for providing care have potential for flourishing and fulfilment, while others should be changed or become obsolete. What works and why? Where is love to be found, and how can it be valued in a world of economics?

Homes, friends and families

'Nearly everyone I met used the concept of family as a main reference point when describing their feelings…they spoke of "family bonds", "we are a family and we support each other", and relationships that "they would never have had on their own so it's like another family"'(Woodward & Kartupelis, 2018, p. 57). Describing the NewBridge retirement community in Boston, Gawande says there are private rooms and a common living area 'like a home' (p. 129) with 'both privacy and community …for the possibility of forming caring relationships' (ibid., p. 131).

Homes and families can to an extent be re-created, both as an emotional and a physical environment, and family-type bonds sustained by facilitation and mediation. However, not all families are happy, and as a paradigm, it demands vigilance to be kept healthy, especially on the part of the project co-ordinator or manager, whose role is considered below.

Although so many interviewees in both community-based and residential groups spoke warmly of having a 'family' again, there can be other drawbacks to the paradigm: for some people (younger carers included) their earlier experiences of family may have been unhappy or dysfunctional, there could have been estrangement or conflict and the concept may raise issues for them.

Another problem arises in care settings if their director or owner exploits the model – a concern explored in detail by Dodson and Zincavage in relation to US institutions in their article 'It's like a family': managers were looking for care staff who would do older people's shopping 'in their own time' and were 'willing to go more than the eight hours' (2007, p. 914). In this scenario, carers (generally female, often black or immigrant workers) were encouraged to see residents as 'kin', and 'the traditional family model of women putting dependent people before other considerations was strongly rooted at all levels of these facilities' (ibid., p. 917) with deleterious effects on the staff in financial and emotional terms.

'Maintaining existing friendships as well as developing supportive friendships with other residents is important for residents and should be encouraged' (*My Home Life*, 2007, p. 29). Friendships may be at the heart of re-created families, but less close relationships can be just as important: 'Relationships that are apparently quite casual and by no means intimate can be a source of emotional support and security' (Barnes et al., 2018, p. 101). Friendships may or may not be very close, as we will see in future chapters, but whatever their nature, they are nurtured by the same type of environment that favours the creation of family bonds.

Reciprocity and 'contribution'

A relationship cannot be one-way if it is to flourish and be supportive. Relationships of care may appear to be all 'give' or all 'take', but this is unsustainable. Gawande describes an elderly couple: 'He found great purpose in caring for her, and she, likewise, found great meaning in being there for him' (2014, p. 86). Of course, one might say, they were a loving married pair; it cannot be the same with paid carers. This would be to misunderstand the nature of work, and the importance within the work setting of engagement, reward and purpose, provided only that the payment is fair and there is support and appreciation to balance the intensity of the 'give'. Reward and support are not just duties of the employer but are found in interactions within the network of older people, carers, managers and families.

Love needs reciprocity to keep it alive, and if one person feels unloved or unknown as an individual, the value of relational interaction is lost. Referring to her book *Caring and Social Justice* (2006), Barnes says that she offered

> a nuanced account of the factors influencing the way caring relationships develop [and] also unsettle[d] the distinction between caregivers and care receivers … encompass[ing] accounts of ways in which they and others had received care from those they care for.
>
> *(Barnes et al., 2018, p. 39)*

Similarly, considering the spiritual aspect of care, Mowat and Mowat emphasise 'the relationship between … carer and cared-for is two way. *We care for each other*' (2018, p. 81, their italics).

Again, reciprocity can be perverted for gain and must be ethically guided, or less than ethical management will see it in terms of 'the bottom line', as Dodson and Zincavage note; they observed that carers found 'the emotional challenge of fulfilling the expectations of a dozen "grandparents" was sometimes overwhelming' (2007, p. 915).

Management and facilitation

Managers of projects or homes set the tone and help to create a space in which people can interact when they wish and equally enjoy peaceful time. This is in part about their awareness of what is happening in the environment they are helping to create, how they themselves participate and how they facilitate others.

Community-based and organisational chaplaincy can also complement the managerial role by facilitating relationships and giving additional time for listening and interpreting need, with the further offering of spiritual support. Some chaplains may be church based or linked to faith groups, such as the Christian Anna Chaplains, working in care homes, private homes, churches and community groups and being there just as much for people of strong, little or no faith. Some may be embedded in providers such as MHA Homes and the Abbeyfield

Society, where they can help each community they visit 'strengthen its internal bonds' (Woodward and Kartupelis, 2018, p. 87). They hold a unique position in being both part of the structure yet separate from it, and their presence can assist relational care but 'the role of the residents in helping build community was vital [with] the chaplain as interlocutor' (Mowat, 2014, p. 18).

However, it is the embedded manager whose function is critical in ensuring a mutual network of support. 'They (the residents) are touched by business hands ... Carla (the manager) though, touches them when it's not necessary and with pure affection ... Her experience and kindness show in the respectful yet intimate affection with which she approaches them' (Hugo, 2005, p. 5). My co-author and I concluded: 'One of the most notable findings of the research was the critical role of the managers, and a number of the respondents described them as the "hub" of the home, or even its "soul"' (Woodward and Kartupelis, 2018, p. 58).

Safety and security

Feeling safe is a basic human need, and one that must be fulfilled in any type of care provision; yet there must also be the space to flourish. These are not mutually exclusive, but ensuring the latter means allowing people as much autonomy as possible. So there must also be an element of risk-taking on the part of the provider. If risk is sensibly assessed and mitigated where it can be without heavily compromising freedom (we will see some examples later of how this has been achieved), it remains an acceptable part of life.

Security is rather different: it is both an emotional and a practical issue about 'someone being there for you', and feeling known, accepted and part of a stable community. Without security, it is harder to establish trust and good relationships – one of the reasons why continuity of care is so critical and why staff turnover and elder frailty are issues. Security was frequently cited by residents and staff as absolutely vital during the Abbeyfield interviews, although it also applies to non-residential settings.

Dignity and respect

Mutual respect is an essential factor in healthy relationships. It expresses itself not only in the overarching philosophy of any setting of care but also in many small ways which can be observed on a daily basis. To take just one example: carers being aware of the appearance of older people, enabling them to choose their clothes for the day, to have their own clothes returned from the laundry and not appropriated by others, to feel clean and odour-free and ready to welcome friends or family. Hugo writes so sadly of meeting a resident in Golden View 'whose hair appears to be combed in a wind tunnel and who wears a battered blue print dress with a sweater so old that it's completely devoid of both colour and shape'. This is a woman whose request for a cup of coffee is being completely ignored by three staff 'perhaps fifteen feet away' (2005, p. 42). She also recounts someone who can no longer retain her dignity by

dressing herself and has been left in 'a shapeless once-white blouse, gray sweatpants…
an old outgrown perm.…battered sneakers' (ibid., p. 117).

Or another example in residential settings: 'people often raised with me …. the
importance of bathroom design and maintenance to dignity and respect.' Communal facilities needing space and hoists 'need to be carefully sited so that people do not
have a long trek in a dressing gown' (Woodward and Kartupelis, 2018, p. 79).

Privacy and company

Part of showing mutual respect, both to older people and to carers and managers, is to ensure they can access privacy when they need to. This is facilitated
by attitudes of awareness and by the built environment. In community settings
such as day care or lunch clubs, it means not dragging people into activities with
overwhelming jocularity, being conscious that they may be feeling fragile, in
need of a quiet chat or of none at all; it also means arranging a large room with
some discreet seating for conversation, and books, puzzles and so on being scat-
tered around. In residential settings, personal space and individual rooms must
be respected, and privacy created in numerous ways that we will look at later in
detail; this applies to privacy for carers as well as for residents.

However, privacy must be balanced by opportunities for company whenever
it is sought, or there will be little interaction and bonding. These environmental
factors are two sides of the same coin in favouring relational care.

THE BALANCE BETWEEN PRIVACY AND COMPANY

'It's wonderful to have company but also to have your own space' (resident).
      'There are some people you want to be with and some people you don't
want to be with. We're lucky we've formed a little social group' (residents).
      'We had a lady who didn't want to attend any meetings or activities and
it was important to respect that' (manager).
      'You have people to chat to whenever you want?' 'Unless they don't chat
back' (interviewer/resident).
      'Some people like to be alone occasionally, but not always' (older client).
      'We like people to be involved, but it's not for everyone; that's their
choice' (owner).
      'You can't force people to join in, but you can help them if they're new'
(care assistant).
      '[At times of bereavement] staff need somewhere private to shed a few
tears' (care worker).
      'When you're isolated it's not good. Just having the company is wonder-
ful' (resident).

The built and physical environment

'To live in a beautiful room, a cosy place …. Will give them meaning, [and] keep people alive' (Jewell, 2004, p. 117); 'wellbeing interacts with, but is not dependent on, material circumstances and can be enhanced or reduced by ….. physical environments' (Barnes et al., 2018, p. 107). It so follows that the physical setting of any care provision will be critical to the formation of supportive relationships, and the models discussed in this book are all considered in terms of these factors: what do they look like, and how do they feel? 'A resident in Woodbridge rejoiced in the characterful buildings, showed us the fine views from her room' (Levy et al., 2017, pages unnumbered). Are there places where people can be comfortable with themselves and others, where they feel they belong and have a stake in that community? What makes them work?

Gardens and getting outdoors

Being in nature and the fresh air is as important as having the right indoors setting and can literally breathe new life into people, animating them to talk to others and build new friendships. Gardening projects in the community, exercise and walking, outings to parks and garden centres, disability- and dementia-friendly gardens, summerhouses and meeting places: all are factors in relational care, and we will look later at their role in the models described.

Even when being outdoors becomes challenging, 'views from windows over the garden, and from the gardens into the landscape beyond, are not only uplifting, but …. Help to keep a connectedness to community and past life' (Woodward and Kartupelis, 2018, p. 53). Conversely, in the home Hugo visited, 'the windows are set too high for residents to see more than the sky…like a perverse miracle, the weather [indoors] is perfectly consistent: seasonless gray' (2005, p. 28). It does not have to be like that, and whatever the age of the building, physical surroundings can be improved.

Sharing meals

The original meaning of companionship – the sharing of bread – indicates the vital importance of eating with others to individual wellbeing (including appetite) and flourishing relationships. Whether it is the coming together from different parts of a town for a daily or weekly lunch as part of team support or a regular mealtime in a home, food has such a range of vital functions in the relational life. It gives opportunities for interaction, for stimulating memories and sharing stories or just listening; it provides nutrition to brain and body; it enables discreet monitoring of each individual's wellbeing; it provides a structure to the day and the week; and of course it can be a source of great enjoyment.

THE JOYS OF SHARING FOOD

'Family mealtimes are very different from restaurant mealtimes. We want to get that right, so the place is beautiful but people also feel beautiful; it's getting that balance' (team co-ordinator).

We want to use meals as a social time, maybe get people with similar interests to sit together' (care worker).

'We like chatty times, lots of afternoon teas, with proper fine china cups and saucers, a tablecloth, a proper afternoon tea' (housekeeper).

Interaction with children and young people

The relationship between children and grandparents is often very special, and the idea of children and older people coming together in care settings has also become increasingly popular, thanks in part to pioneering work being featured on television. Intergenerational projects will be explored in detail in Chapter 4, but it should also be remembered that there can be a less structured presence of youngsters in almost any care setting, and when there is, it is generally beneficial to all and is another factor that nurtures a range of supportive relationships and more fulfilled life.

THE COMPANY OF CHILDREN

'Do you bring your children in?' 'Yes, they [older people] don't want to give them back!' (interviewer/carer).

'My youngest son comes in; he's 16, he makes them laugh. It's very family oriented here' (carer).

'My grandson has formed a relationship with one of the residents – it just seemed to come about – he's a caring little boy' (office manager).

'Local people and the school bring their children and pets in; the older generation love the younger generation' (manager).

'He doesn't get upset if they get his name wrong. Children seem to appreciate what older people can and can't do' (parent).

The company of animals

For those who have loved pets, or farmed, or lived in the countryside, a life without animals can be sterile. The health benefits of pets have long been documented (e.g., stroking a cat while it purrs rhythmically reduces heart rate and blood pressure; a University of Toronto study found that dog owners have a

24% reduced risk of dying in any year), but the emotional benefits are also well recognised.

> Pets provide another opportunity for older people to give attention and affection, while also providing comfort and a topic for conversation. Several studies have identified the positive impact of pets on residents' well-being …. One recent study, for example, found a significant, positive change in mood for those receiving visits from volunteers with a dog compared with a visitor alone (Lutwack–Bloom et al., 2005).
>
> *(My Home Life, p. 74)*

'Talking about who they were and still are inside lights a revival fire that warms them and holds back the dark… my dog, with her silky ears and eager tongue and shiny, caressable coat… coaxes out their buried selves' (Hugo, 2005, p. 17); as they spend time together the dog, her owner and the older person are 'looking for purpose, extracting meaning, coaxing out joy' (ibid., p. 16). The presence of animals not only evokes memories and calms anxiety but also becomes a catalyst for conversation, and for many people, it is another critical factor in contentment, flourishing and being open to forming new bonds.

The 11 points above are all key environmental factors in creating the criteria for relational care, against which different models will be assessed in the following chapters; in part by reference to evaluation reports, but primarily through descriptions of real-life examples of models, and the observations and words of those participating in them.

Relational care and the role of carers

Care delivery environments other than the family are shared by older people and paid carers, but the focus of aspiration and improvement is so often on the former rather than the latter. Yet if the reciprocity and benefits of relational care are going to thrive, then both groups, as well as visitors and volunteers, must be supported. Fortunately, in terms of the critical factors summarised above, what is good for one is normally good for all.

An Office for National Statistics (ONS) report in January 2020 noted that the occupational sector 'care workers and home carers' was the second largest in the UK in 2018/2019, comprising 781,500 workers. Enabling these people to be their best for themselves and others represents a major ethical and practical challenge. Meyer argues that promoting 'relationship centred care, both as a therapeutic intervention and positive environment for learning' demands an 'understanding that individual, team and organisational health is interdependent' (*My Home Life*, p. 134).

The relational role of care staff

Whether operating in a community or in a residential setting, carers in a relational network are both partners and facilitators, helping in the search to 'write a meaningful conclusion' (Jewell, 2004, p. 122) to life but also being part of that life meaning. They are known and valued by older people and vice versa, but at the same time, they can enable bonds to be strengthened with families and built with new friends. This can happen in part if they are able to restore control to those at risk of being disenfranchised by age, to 'pull out the stinger of powerlessness' (Hugo, 2005, p. 42) and dare to become attached themselves 'in order to help residents preserve autonomy and control' (ibid., p. 55). And also in part if they can catalyse links to families by being 'welcoming and hospitable for visitors, and responding to their needs' (Meyer in *My Home Life,* p. 29) because 'Staying involved [for families] means establishing new relationships with staff, and with other residents and their families' (ibid., p. 67).

What this implies for their support needs

Demands are made on carers in terms of time, emotional involvement and hard physical work; as Mowat says, it is a tough job: 'care staff who are dealing with difficult emotions and situations on a daily basis have their own struggles. They are too busy, too harassed, poorly paid and usually juggling busy family life with their caring roles' (2014, p. 29). 'This is not about bad people who don't care, and if it's cast that way, it masks the real needs' (Hugo, p. 58). Gallagher makes the point that abusive behaviour can arise from the devaluation of caregivers, which is a systemic rather than individual matter and makes 'Caring for the caregivers … an important priority' (Scott ed., 2017, Chapter 15, p. 8).

This is work, and hard work at that, but it is also not *just* work. A study of relationships in care homes cited in *My Home Life* (2007, p67) 'found close relationships between residents and staff and suggested that lack of attachment was a strong predictor of staff burnout and turnover (Sumaya-Smith 1995)' and 'with consistent staff assignment, relationships can flourish leading to improved quality of care and lower staff turnover' (ibid.). Care staff have the same basic spiritual needs as older people: to feel loved, to be affirmed, to have moments of tranquillity and to have faith in their life meaning and purpose.

This is the challenge that managers and care workers in all settings face: the extent to which they can be involved while at the same time maintaining a separate family and personal life. As one carer said: 'I love my job but I also have small children. People need me here and people need me at home.' And yet, we do not ask this question when an individual enjoys a range of friendships, emotional involvements and family ties. Most of us expect to value different types of relationship at different times and in various places as part of life's richness. If some of those relationships are to be found in a paid environment, there will be no problem as long as 'employment' does not equate to 'exploitation', and society and policy makers do not dismiss carers as 'low skilled' or transient but as one of the most important work sectors in our shared life.

The more salient observation is that in 'normal' life we tend not to lose loved ones frequently, whereas carers of frail ageing people will encounter loss of someone they have grown to love on a more regular basis; and at the same time, they have to deal professionally and empathetically with family and other residents encountering the same loss. The question is how carers can be helped through difficult times, and as we will see, the answer again lies in relationships of support.

Being valued and feeling valued by older people, families and their employers for who they are *and* for what they do is essential: 'it is necessary to understand care as a value as well as a practice, [but] those values are literally embodied in how bodies are handled and addressed as their frailties become exposed' (Barnes et al., 2018, p. 36). While it is true that 'the relational aspects of care must be rewarded, both monetarily and spiritually' in order to motivate carers in terms of 'non-instrumental tasks' (Cluff and Binstock, 2001, p. 173), it is more productive (and time efficient) to think of both the loving and practical tasks being all part of one and the same 'give'. How this can be assisted to happen will be discussed later.

Time is indeed an issue, and one of the main problems of which carers speak is feeling forever rushed. This not only creates pressure and stress for employees, inhibiting relationships that could support them and older people, but also leads to 'task-centred' delivery, worse care outcomes and disregarding what is actually needed: 'In the time-starved environments characteristic of many care homes, it is easier and faster to assume what an older person would like than to truly establish their wishes' (Davies and Brown-Wilson in *My Home Life*, 2007, p. 87). Sufficient time is one of the most important things any employer of care workers can provide to support health and happiness, and this has financial implications for care provision, which are discussed in the final chapter.

Once relationships become established, less maintenance time is needed, making not only for a happier situation but also for a cost-effective one. Continuity of care is both a moral and economic imperative, and it is amazing that some care providers, and some central policies, give so little priority to staff retention.

Envisaging the future in terms of relational care

Neither people nor care provision can ever be perfect, but it is very possible to find examples of places and projects that largely adhere to most if not all of the key criteria and hence environmental factors described above. Some started that way; others adapted (through additional support to people, modifying structures, adding refinements) and developed by changing focus and priorities and then carried on when they saw the benefits.

This book covers a wide variety of good practice and innovation but has chosen not to focus on care settings that already have a wealth of information available about their particular category; this includes particularly dementia care and care by blood relatives and spouses, or within 'genetic' families. The choice of models, the methodology of the studies and a list of useful resources pertaining to the omitted categories can be found in Appendix B.

All the examples in this book have ideas to offer. Some raise as well as answer questions; some needed a lot of financial investment and others none; some may seem easy and others hardly achievable – but they have been achieved through inspiration, hard work and vision.

Trusting in the concept of relational care can challenge accepted ideas about older people, about the type of care they want and what matters to them, about the role of their families and carers, about the real purpose of care and the institutions that provide it and about whose responsibility it all is anyway. However, the people and places described in the following chapters suggest some fresh ways of meeting the challenges and may even bring a little inspiration!

Some further reading related to this chapter

Listening to older people

There are a number of books based on conversations with older people and careful listening, for example: Elizabeth MacKinlay's work, *The Spiritual Dimension of Ageing* (2001, Jessica Kingsley), *Re-imagining Old Age* (Barnes et al., 2018, Vernon Press), *Valuing Age* (Woodward, 2008, SPCK) and *Age Speaks for Itself* (Koch, 2000, Praeger).

Care ethics

This concept and its history are described in detail in Chapter 15 by Gallagher in *Key Concepts in Nursing Ethics* (Scott, P.A. ed., 2017, Springer) and in Chapter 2 in *Re-imagining Old Age* (Barnes et al., 2018, Vernon Press).

The Butterfly Approach model of care

Described by David Sheard on the Dementia Care Matters web site: www.dementiacarematters.com

Pet therapy

Where the Trail Grows Faint (Hugo, 2005), University of Nebraska Press, is a moving and insightful personal account by novelist Lynne Hugo of a year in the life of a therapy dog team working in a US care home for older people.

The spiritual aspects of care

MHA (Methodist Homes for the Aged) Care Group provides training programmes for staff and leadership through conferences and seminars in this field. The Leveson Centre provides a focus for interdisciplinary study of ageing, spirituality and social policy through publications, seminars, conferences, research and networking.

The concept of meaning in life

An overview is given in 'Meaning in life of older persons: An integrative literature review' (Hupkens et al., *Nursing Ethics*, December 2016).

The concepts of wellbeing and resilience

'Wellbeing or resilience: Blurred encounters between theory and practice' (Reader, J.) in *The Practices of Happiness: Political Economy, Religion and Wellbeing* edited by Atherton, Graham and Steedman (2010, Routledge).

Gestalt theory

For the history and practice of this, see https://gestaltcentre.org.uk/what-is-gestalt/

2

CREATING RELATIONAL CARE MODELS IN COMMUNITY SETTINGS

History and development of community-based care for older people

It is axiomatic that an indicator of a civilised society is its willingness to look after and protect its most vulnerable members, but that axiom begs many questions about overall capacity and priorities. Who will look after whom, and who will pay? Are there any limitations? As we have seen when considering the recent history of social care in the previous chapter, ways of providing for those in need and interpretations of need are very variable at different times and in different places. This chapter first considers how non-residential care of older people has been and is currently provided in the UK, and then it looks in detail at some models that foster relational care and their salient features.

The great majority of older people in the UK live in their own homes, a higher proportion than in the United States, but this may well change. A survey undertaken in 2016 (Laing and Buisson) found that the number of people living in specialist retirement housing or in care homes is relatively low: approximately 416,000 people live in care, which represents 4% of the population aged 65 years and over, rising to 16% of those aged 85 or more. Not everyone over 65 or even 85 requires some type of care provision, of course. However, people aged 65 and over are a large and rapidly growing group, as indicated by the figures given in the previous chapter.

While it is true that 'From the dawn of human history, of course, families… have been the major source of caring for their sick and disabled relatives' (Cluff and Binstock, 2001, p. 5), this has never been a full answer to the social challenge (there may not be relatives present or willing or able) and is even less so today when people are more geographically dispersed and have multiple demands on their time. However, there remains a general assumption that care within the community ought to be possible and is generally desirable, in comparison to residential care.

> The vast majority of the care received by older people continues to be provided by friends and relatives. In 2015–16, 8 per cent of the population, or just fewer than 5 million people, were informal carers (Department for Work and Pensions, 2017). Over a third (35.7 per cent) of unpaid carers provided care for over 100 hours per week (NHS Digital, 2017).
>
> *(Cottell, 2017, p. 9)*

While many carers do find their role rewarding and have freely made the choice to take it on, others may have more mixed feelings about the emotional and physical demands, and the very substantial time input.

Local Authorities (LAs) in England, Scotland and Wales and Local Commissioning Boards in Northern Ireland have a statutory duty to provide social care to meet the needs of older people whose assets fall below a certain level, and in theory, if friends and family did not step in, all the obligations would fall to them; and as we will see in Chapter 6, LAs are already struggling under major financial burdens.

Non-residential care can be provided as home care, or in sheltered housing and co-living schemes, where older owners and renters choose whether and what type of care they wish to have supplied (which may or may not be LA funded). For the purposes of this chapter, the focus will be on schemes offering home care or 'care at home' (visits by carers to an individual's own home) and projects with a community base, such as a day care centre, meeting points or provision of outings. These may be provided by the LA or by private or third-sector organisations, and they may be funded by the LA, privately or charitably. Also, this chapter does not cover care provided informally by friends or relatives, not because it is unimportant – quite the contrary – but because there is already a great deal of literature available addressing issues about and advising on that sector.

'Extra care' schemes, which generally comprise self-contained ('own front door') homes that are leased by individuals but have some communal facilities and on-site care available, will be considered in Chapter 3, together with care homes. While lessors often have low care needs initially, these are likely to increase with time, eventually becoming significantly higher but possibly still at a threshold lower than nursing care.

The legislation and changes in provision that led to the creation of care institutions were traced in the previous chapter, but institutions never became the norm for ageing care in the UK, and this remains the case. The alms houses movement stretches back many centuries, and while alms houses were and are not care homes, they do provide an interesting model that may be developed in new ways – one of which features in Chapter 4. Any care provided to their residents would originally have come from family, neighbours and the church.

The concept of a neighbourhood in which people were well known to one another, and the needs of the more vulnerable were apparent, has been steadily eroded by changes in society, such as the movement of people, the nature of working life and the growth of large settlements with transient residents. These changes have their roots in the Industrial Revolution, and also in philosophies of individualism and liberalism; however, they can be over-stated, and there still remain in Britain many small settlements (villages, market towns, areas of large cities) where there is a thriving 'neighbourhood', just as there are also streets where no-one knows their neighbour's name.

Without wishing to romanticise the past, the benefits of a neighbourhood can be recreated, and Barnes et al. found this to be happening naturally when they interviewed older people in Brighton; respondents talked about

> the importance of neighbours who knew who they were, would be aware if they didn't appear or open their curtains, and who would pop in from time to time... it is the nature of the relationship between old people and those who might, in different ways be keeping an eye on them, that can make the difference in terms of retaining a sense of wellbeing related to security or experiencing an invasion of privacy that can undermine wellbeing.
>
> *(2018, p. 138)*

The benefits and problems of care delivered within the community

> Opportunities for people to remain socially active and engaged within their communities, with valued roles and status...may contribute to tackling depression more than the array of help from social services... it may also encourage continued physical activity, delaying or minimising the onset of deterioration.
>
> *(Woodward, 2008 p. 186)*

There is no doubt that living in a supportive neighbourhood has the potential to meet many of the key criteria for relational care: bonds of friendship and possibly family, being known and accepted, having access to company and privacy, being able to eat with others (perhaps through church, community centre, invitations, dropping in on people for coffee and so on), interaction with young people and animals, health care with relative ease if there is a GP surgery in the neighbourhood and using grocery delivery services. If many or all of these are available, then staying 'independent' (a term that is actually quite complex and 'loaded' and will be explored in the next chapter) is very possible.

But for many older people, this is just a dream, and they are in the position of having to rely in full or part on visits from care and health workers. What of supportive relational care in that situation: is it possible? The answer is a qualified 'yes', and the models presented below will show how it can be achieved, but it is worth looking first at the issues that have to be tackled.

Cluff and Binstock warn:

> Despite evidence to the contrary, a steadfast belief… in the cost-effectiveness of noninstitutional long term care has led to a shift towards formal, paid caregiving services in the home and other community settings… [this] has given rise to institutional structures and controls that often undermine the norms of caring. For example, home care agencies often advise their employees not to get too emotionally attached to their clients.
>
> *(2001, p. 246)*

However, this 'steadfast belief' is not just to do with cost but is also firmly held in terms of there being benefits to older people in keeping them in their own homes for as long as possible. The older people involved are likely to feel strongly that this is what they themselves want, but in some cases, this tenacity to home is based on misplaced fears and misconceptions, as we will see later.

The term 'care at home' covers a range of personal services, such as assistance with dressing, meals and hygiene and may be paid for privately or by a Local Authority (LA) (buying in private agency services as necessary) or a combination of the two. Where LAs are very short of money, clients may be 'downgraded' in their assessment as requiring only voluntary help, which could be excellent or non-existent. Health care at home is a different matter, provided by nurses and falling under the aegis of the NHS. Frailer older people may well need both services, and if they are living in suitable housing with a spouse or other family, the arrangement can work well. But problems arise if the older person is living alone or in unsuitable accommodation that cannot be, or is too expensive to be, adapted.

> The worst scenario is a decline into almost total lack of company… The final indignity is the frail older person put to bed in the early evening during the final visit of the carer that day, wrapped in an adult nappy to see out the night.
>
> *(Woodward and Kartupelis, 2018, p. 120)*

One of the major problems is the nature of care visits, which are likely to be rushed in situations where workers try to adhere to near-impossible schedules dictated by limited funding. Also, because there may be personal and nursing care needs, the chances are that there will be a variety of different carers involved. There is little time to get to listen to and know their clients, and this is exacerbated if there are changes of staff who

> are often employed on part-time or zero hours contracts… may receive little in the way of regular supervision or support, and who operate within severe constraints on the amount of time they can spend before moving on to their next client.
>
> *(Barnes et al., 2018, p. 180)*

This may not be so true where clients have sufficient funding of their own and can choose private provision that offers consistency and choice, but it remains the scenario for many.

Barnes et al. cover these problems in depth in *Re-imagining Old Age*, warning that older people have little contact with professional social workers and their main relationships are with 'front-line care workers [who] have little opportunity themselves for relational support … some of the lowest paid workers, with the worst terms and conditions, they are often faced with trying to meet complex human demands without adequate resources' (ibid., p. 180). They conclude that 'drawing on personal experience … we know that ethical relational practice can be provided by care workers in this context, but generally this is only because individual workers are willing to pay the high personal cost' (ibid., p. 181). This observation echoes disturbingly those of Dodson and Zincavage, that encouraging 'kinship' and good relational care can at its worst slide into exploitation.

Loneliness

One of the curses of modern Western society is the prevalence of loneliness, and this is a key issue where delivery of, and moving from, care in the community to other settings are concerned.

Loneliness is a subjective experience, insofar as it is felt by the individual as a deficit in relationships, a gap between what they would find ideal and their actual perceived situation. In this respect it is different from social isolation, which is an objective state. It is perfectly possible to feel lonely when surrounded by people or, conversely, to be quite content alone if it is one's chosen state. This phenomenon can be explained in part by a tendency to feeling lonely being 50% influenced by inherited genetic factors as well as 50% by the prevailing environment.

Loneliness affects all age groups and genders.

> In 2016 to 2017, there were 5% of adults in England who reported feeling lonely 'often' or 'always'. Younger adults aged 16 to 24 years reported feeling lonely more often than those in older age groups. Women reported feeling lonely more often than men.
> *(ONS, 10.4.18, www.ons.gov.uk ›peoplepopulationandcommunity › wellbeing › articles)*

It is particularly concerning that 'loneliness can be as harmful for our health as smoking 15 cigarettes a day, and people with a high degree of loneliness are twice as likely to develop Alzheimer's as people with a low degree of loneliness' (Davidson and Rossall, 2015, Age UK, p. 3). Measuring subjective states is always challenging (see Appendix A), and the methods of measuring loneliness are based on accepted scales of wellbeing (ibid., p. 4 onwards).

There are recognised risk factors for loneliness in older age: 'In the UK Dahlberg and McKee (2014) reported that loneliness in later life is associated with being widowed, having low self-esteem, contacts with friends or family, social activity, well-being, and income comfort; and having unmet social care needs' (*Predicting the Prevalence of Loneliness at Older Ages*, Iparraguirre, undated, Age UK). A number of these factors are the opposite of the key criteria for relational care, which is based on increasing autonomy and confidence, creating interdependence and encouraging meaningful activity.

However, a higher proportion of older people in care homes report feeling lonely than those living in their own family homes (Davidson and Rossall, 2015, p. 7), which could suggest the need for a different approach or environment in care homes, though this is not proven. Certainly as the voices quoted below evidence, it is possible to create environments that address loneliness and greatly improve wellbeing. 'Key transitions' (ibid., p. 8) can also trigger loneliness and may be a factor in feeling lonely in a new residential setting. This argues for such transitions being handled very carefully, as discussed later in this chapter, and in this respect, community-based care teams have an important role to play.

CREATING ENVIRONMENTS THAT ADDRESS LONELINESS

'Someone will move into care and they don't want to come out of their room. If we don't encourage or find out what they're interested in, that's where you get the situation in care where people become socially isolated' (manager).

'Here there's 24 hours support whereas home care is just people going in, boredom and depression' (care assistant).

'I was here early in the year for three weeks respite and when I went back to my flat I felt so lonely, so moved back here permanently. There's always company here, someone to talk to' (resident).

'The team are encouraged to address social isolation. It's not just that someone feels a bit lonely. There are massive implications' (activities co-ordinator).

'Care in the community isn't about putting someone in front of the television, but often individuals have no other choice. They've been told you have 15 minutes in the morning, half an hour at lunch and in the evening' (manager who had worked in domiciliary care).

Favouring relational care: team-based models of provision

'Care at home' and community-based care, especially in combination where necessary, have the potential to provide good relational care in the right setting. They also have the potential to leave older people trapped in their own homes, lonely and unknown. We will now look at some models that address the disadvantages and maximise the benefits, how they have worked and what learning points they offer.

Neighbourhood Cares teams

The nature of the scheme

Neighbourhood Cares (NC) is a scheme established by Cambridgeshire County Council, in response to their recognition that conventional domiciliary care comes with a number of problems; not only those noted above but also that it is expensive and can be inefficient. Their response has been to set up two pilot teams, both in towns of around 10,000 population, designed and resourced to act as a community asset, give continuity of relationships and test an adaptation of the Buurtzorg model described later. The teams operate from St Ives, a market town with outlying suburban development, and Soham, a rural town; this case study is about the Soham team.

The teams were established in October 2017 and were monitored and assessed over two years, internally by the County Council and externally by York Consulting. The teams were self-managed on the Buurtzorg principle and initially comprised four senior workers in each, although they grew to add more junior members. The aim was to provide preventative, flexible and responsive care within the local community, moving away from a system of separate, specialist county-wide teams with a reliance on statutory assessments and remotely commissioned care and at the same time making community connections and building assets.

Clients, who are not only older people but also others with physical or mental health needs, were referred by existing services such as GPs and could also self-refer. Some required long-term assistance, even until death in some cases, and others needed bridging help, for example during a change of circumstance. The Soham team has worked with well over 350 clients since its inception, around half of which were already known to other adult social care teams, with cases being transferred from the Older Peoples and Physical Disabilities Teams. NC also worked with partners including health services, voluntary bodies and other providers.

The pilot scheme was funded by the County Council; they and the teams decided against setting up a separate body, such as a Social Enterprise. Although the project established a new structure for health and social services to work together, the Council also decided against seeking NHS funding, as it preferred to retain control of the project rather than it becoming a health service adjunct.

The objectives of the original business case made to establish NC were to:

- Shift as much resource as possible to the front line
- Free up staff to have more direct contact with people enabling them to do the best job and improve job satisfaction
- Improve the quality and continuity of care and support to people
- Increase capacity where there are currently gaps, particularly in home care
- Reduce the cost of care
- Learn from the pilot sites to form the basis for the wider transformation of the whole system

What Neighbourhood Cares looks like

Soham is a rural town, with facilities such as shops, schools, churches and a library that includes community rooms. I visited them there four times, to meet the team, sit in on part of its meetings, join in a coffee morning and interview four clients privately in depth. The sections that follow are drawn from my own experience and interviews; the York Consulting Interim Evaluation; and County Council documents, to which I was given access.

The NC team used the library as its base and mentioned that having the Soham library as the team's base has been beneficial in terms of foot fall and access to a range of meeting spaces. [We] have been able to use the building during and outside of normal opening times. A common response from people attending events we run here is 'I have not been in the building since I was at school. I will now come in again it's got such a welcoming atmosphere'. York noted that it was 'an existing hub for community activity and a safe, non-threatening space (York, 2018, p. 5).

Location is important, as the NC concept is based on the idea of face-to-face meetings in the hub and in people's homes, to give continuity and be able to monitor whole-life situations. 'Once those trusting relationships are established clients were more willing to engage with other professionals, such as GPs or mental health professionals, which previously they had been reluctant to do' (ibid, p. 13). Trust is built partly by the speed of response which a basically autonomous team can offer (as long as it has the capacity) as 'they are not constrained by timeframes in a way that other services are' (ibid., p. 12), and in turn this gives more autonomy to its clients, who have more time to make decisions and become less anxious waiting, so feel more in control of their care. A critical factor is that teams and clients build relationships before a point of crisis is reached so 'clients are managing crises better because they have the strategies in place to address them … [this] helps to establish trusting relationships going forward' (ibid., p. 11).

Impacts

Looking in from the outside, at the relationships between team members, their grasp of situations and events and the interactions between clients, it was clear that trust had been built not only with individuals but with the families of which they were part. It is therefore not so surprising to find that the way the team works has such an impact, to the point of saving lives:

> Partners were clear that without the involvement of NC teams, some of their clients would not have sought help for the issues they faced, would not have been supported by other professionals and would have died. This view was also reiterated by clients we spoke to.
>
> *(Ibid., p. 23)*

They have also had an impact on the wider community. The teams met people who would not qualify for support from social workers and helped them with information about sources of assistance; as a result of their work:

> A wide range of community assets have been developed, including: a re-pairs café, a coffee and cake club, monthly pub lunches, informal drop-in sessions, bi-monthly community newsletter…. and the delivery of an inter-generational project …. The community assets developed have been based on what people said they would like.
>
> *(Ibid., p. 28)*

These also include a community map of activities and enabling opportunities for volunteers.

The internal and external evaluation studies indicate benefits for clients, staff and the wider community. York Consultancy, using consultancy, data review and in-depth interviews, concluded that in a relatively short time (around one year) the NC team had become 'a trusted resource' (ibid., p. iii). The NC work was welcomed by partners such as GPs, especially in St Ives, where the team was embedded in a surgery and also stimulated more self-referrals, particularly in Soham, ensuring preventative measures were taken.

One of the original objectives in setting up the pilot project was to assess the impact of the teams on costs, and this is work-in-progress. York Consulting notes, 'Evidencing the impact of long-term preventative support, i.e. preventing crises and what might have happened without NCT input, is clearly a challenge' (p. 23), but it is possible to summarise outcomes noted in their report that would be likely to represent cost savings. These are:

- Improving their confidence and helping clients to support themselves and manage their anxieties has reduced demands on other professionals such as GPs and services such as ambulance call outs
- Support from Neighbourhood Cares has helped clients manage their levels of anxiety and helped to prevent an escalation in their mental health needs
- [The teams] were also ensuring better continuity of care, which it was felt were preventing hospital admissions
- The teams have supported clients to improve their living conditions and address safety issues within the home [through referrals] …. This helps to prevent falls
- Clients have avoided hospital admissions because the teams have been able to respond quickly to a deterioration in clients' health
- By ensuring clients are accessing the benefits to which they are entitled teams have been able to resolve clients' financial difficulties and prevent possible evictions due to rent arrears

An additional impact has subsequently been identified:

• The good foundations laid by the project proved their value during the Coronavirus outbreak in 2020, when the individual bonds and social links that had been established helped in fostering active community support and reference points that people could trust

What does Neighbourhood Cares feel like?

This scheme exemplifies how good relational care can be provided by a community-based team and encouraged in the wider area so that the benefits are optimised. Considering the key criteria for relational care, the voices of those involved, recorded from interviews and quoted from evaluation records, indicate how this scheme makes them feel about the things that matter.

BUILDING RELATIONSHIPS OF TRUST AND BEING KNOWN

'They have become a trusted resource because they have had time to respond and build relationships with clients' (report).

'She [team member] is a resource to help me and she asks me what I want. She's someone who's there for me and on my side' (client).

'It's all about communication and dialogue and I have lovely dialogue with [team member]' (client).

'They are discussing things with us, because we are really developing a relationship with people, rather than just seeing them one or two times' (team member).

'With us, they know us, they develop a relationship with us, that's a huge reassurance to them and their families' (team member).

'They [the team] can tell if you're having a bad day' (client).

'[With a new client] you look for special qualities and draw those out' (volunteer).

'[NC] has made me feel part of something, like I belong' (client).

Enabling greater autonomy and life purpose

'A key part of the NC has been enabling people to act for themselves' (report).

'People like to be cared about, but not to have care done to them' (client).

'It's all about making me stronger and coping on my own. The whole point of it is to empower you' (client).

'What has NC brought to your life?' 'Richness, people, skills and resources' (client).

'I was asked to come and sit on the panel for [staff] interviews, and have become part of the voluntary service' (client/volunteer).

'I now have self-worth which I didn't have for a long time' (client).

Addressing isolation

'The team is working with a number of community groups to ensure that "No one is ever alone in Soham"' (report).

'She was very isolated and struggles to engage, so I made sure she sat with people who would respond to her. She's seeing the benefits' (team member).

'I've known my next-door neighbour for a long time. When I'm on early shifts she'll pop round to see if I'd like a meal cooked. When she's on nights and her husband is ill in the night, he'd call me, and I'll get an ambulance if he needs it' (client of community project).

Building the wider community

'The team is re-energising and re-establishing community groups' (report).

'They'd been going a few months when I got here. It's developed a lot, I've helped set up different groups' (client/volunteer).

'We had nothing before, if this project wasn't here, I don't know what I'd have done' (client).

'I like having more groups and variety in the community' (client).

Benefits to staff

'It allows me to be the social worker I wanted to be' (team member).

'Enabling me to be responsive to people and people's needs and not having to get them to fit into boxes' (team member).

Learning points

The main learning points from the project, for any other organisation considering a similar approach, can be summarised as follows (sources in brackets).

For the managing organisation:

- It is essential to invest time. It takes time to get it set up and get it right: to recruit the right people, provide induction, put the right recording system in place, let the team form and build internal trust ('critical to facilitating effective set up of the teams' York, p. 6)
- Continue to allow the team sufficient time. The way they need to work, with quick responses and longer-term interventions to build relationships,

and the way they need to develop and take others on board, as well as the back office tasks, demands capacity (internal evaluation and York p. iv)

- Trust the team. They need a high level of autonomy, and to be able to move outside existing systems (York p. iii)
- Give the team control of client budgets. They need to be able to control client budgets, otherwise they cannot be truly self-managed, client-centred, flexible and innovative (York, p. iii)
- Find a suitable community building. One that is not forbidding or hard to access, with one large and at least one smaller room available, flexible opening hours, and good IT (internal evaluation)

For the team:

- The team as an entity should be generalist, but each member should be a specialist. Start with senior people, then add more junior members later, and reablement workers (internal evaluation)
- Make sure every client has a named contact. But enable them to access other people as well (York, p. ii)
- Build partner relationships as quickly as possible. NHS, volunteers, community projects, care providers all need to be reassured that the new team will not ask too much of them or duplicate their work (York, p. 8)
- Support volunteers. Harness skills within the client group, identify other volunteers, focus on voluntary work becoming self-sustaining (York, p. 27)
- Avoid clients becoming over-dependent. Do not be tempted to give the early ones unlimited time, or they will not develop their own autonomy (from interviews)
- Build a good recording system. One that captures the evidence you really need, but minimises any unnecessary paperwork (internal evaluation)
- Ensure your work is community wide. Keep people informed, engage volunteers, help new projects start up; these people will then carry some of the work and release your time for development (York, p. i)

Wellbeing teams

The nature of the scheme

This is a nationwide initiative established in 2016 by Helen Sanderson, to provide services to adult clients, who may be older people or have other types of need such as mental health issues. Interestingly, Sanderson says it was particularly inspired by Atul Gawande's book *Being Mortal*, which is cited in the previous chapter, and *Reinventing Organisations* by Frederic Laloux, which talks of bringing the whole self to work, focus on purpose and self-management. Laloux refers to the Buurtzorg model described later in this chapter, as an example rooted in these premises.

Wellbeing Teams are based on the principle of self-managed teams with the objective of supporting and empowering clients in daily care tasks and, most importantly helping them to do more of what matters to them and enjoy active, connected lives independently in their own community.

The project is a social enterprise that may be paid for by a Local Authority or privately; it also provides learning and development to other organisations that want to adopt the same approach. It started with four test sites based in existing organisations, which at this stage highlighted that it was essential for people to buy into the concept of self-management, which some found too alien for their existing culture. Following pilot assessment, teams were set up in Wigan, Thurrock (Kent) and South Oxfordshire; and the concept is spreading to other areas.

The scheme is values-led by:

Compassion: Actively hearing and sensing one another's thoughts and feelings, being kind, and finding empathetic ways to support individuals and each other to achieve positive outcomes.

Responsibility: Initiating ways of working that dignify everyone, at the same time holding self and others accountable for actions and attitudes in relation to our shared purpose and values.

Collaboration: Cooperating with others by sharing ideas and insights to find ways of achieving positive change, both individually and collectively.

Curiosity: Feeling energised by discovering new insights, learning, finding answers to questions and wondering at the world.

Creativity: Capacity and ingenuity to respond appropriately to seize opportunities without needing to be directed or instructed by others.

Flourishing: Creating the conditions for thriving that reflect aspirations, remove barriers to connection and enable people to choose their own way forward.

All these values are predicated on kindness, empathy, dignity, being open to new experiences, contributing to a shared life, finding purpose and, critically, flourishing and growing rather than being diminished by age. In other words, they are very similar to the key criteria for relational care and express themselves not only through the way teams work but also in how they form and sustain themselves.

What Wellbeing Teams look like

Most importantly, teams are relationship-focussed, offering mutual support for clients and for each other, and aim towards giving everyone a 'great day': something to feel good about and a sense of achievement. They are recruited and supported as a single entity, and on their capacity to self-manage. Team members are not normally from a care home background but have worked in various people-oriented organisations; therefore they do not have preconceptions about care delivery but do offer a variety of experience to meet 'head, hands and heart' needs. They are also diverse in terms of age and cultural background. Recruitment is based primarily on competences of compassion and self-responsibility, and people's ability and suitability must be demonstrated over a three-month trial period. The teams use technology carefully, to undertake some tasks with the aim of optimising face-to-face time.

Each client is taken through a 'support sequence' looking at how to get the most out of self-care, assistant technology, input from family and friends and existing community-based schemes. The Wellbeing Team can be seen as a 'central operating system' with a range of optional 'apps' that clients can use as and when required: for example, home care, assistance with daily activities, advice and support on finding suitable work. The benefit is that whatever they need, it can be accessed from a small group of people who are well known to the client and who work closely together. However, they avoid befriending, believing this does not empower people and is too 'one-way'.

A key component of the offering is Circle Family (part of the charity Community Circles), a membership-based programme of local events and activities, to help people to connect around shared interests, creating the conditions for friendship and mutual support. Created as a partnership between Wellbeing Teams, HMR Circle and Community Circles, it acts rather as we have seen the Neighbourhood Cares team doing earlier in this chapter, tapping into and extending existing community resources to the benefit not only of clients but of everyone in a locality.

Impacts

Wellbeing Teams were the first social care provider organisation to be rated Outstanding by the Care Quality Commission, and their programme has had some significant impacts on the development of this type of programme:

- Their value-based recruitment process and innovation provides learning and examples, and is multi-award winning
- They have double the retention rate of equivalent organisations
- They supported people who had not left the house for three to six months to be part of community and social events improving the connections and community activity by over 65%
- They were the first provider to employ a social prescriber

What does being involved with a Wellbeing Team feel like?

This is another scheme that exemplifies how good relational care can be provided by self-managed teams. Considering the key criteria for relational care, the quotes below assist in understanding why the scheme is taking root and growing and has been recognised for its innovative practice in recruitment and delivery.

THE CLIENT EXPERIENCE: BUILDING RELATIONSHIPS AND AUTONOMY

People told us they were partners in their care and had control over what support they had. The service without exception respected people's choices and found innovative and caring ways to both support and protect people in their choices.

People said they knew their wellbeing workers well and that they went above and beyond what would normally be expected of them.

The service put the people they supported and the people who knew them best at the heart of organising and planning care, so that the best outcomes for people were achieved.

(Source: CQC inspection report https://www.cqc.org.uk/location/1-4350577807/reports)

People were actively encouraged to maintain relationships with friends and remain active members of their wider local community and build new relationships. The service signposted people to events being run by other organisations and where a person's interests were not being met, the service tried to arrange activities that would interest the person and link the person with a wellbeing worker who shared the same interest.

(Source: CQC inspection report https://www.cqc.org.uk/location/1-4350577807/reports)

The team experience: building relationships

'Being part of a small self-managing team has allowed me to connect with my colleagues like family.'

'Having a job that is so flexible and enjoyable never feels like 'work'. My colleagues, and those we support never fail to inspire me.'

'We have weekly team meetings so we are able to make decisions to ensure we are offering the best support, share ideas, acknowledge things that have worked/haven't worked well and support each other.'

'I don't feel over-managed or micromanaged which is a fantastic feeling.'

'[The team has] helped progress my career and I became the dementia champion with the team.'

(Source: team members)

The team experience: achievement and validation

'I joined Wellbeing Teams as a student nurse. I have gained confidence and was supported to make decisions and use my initiative. The role has really boosted my confidence.'

'Wellbeing Teams encourages colleagues to reach their potential. I started as a Wellbeing Worker but progressed in a very short time to being a care coordinator (or scheduler) with the support of my team. It has given me so much confidence that I am now thinking about studying to become a nurse.'

'After university, I took up a job as a delivery driver, which wasn't exactly a passion of mine or relevant to my degree. But then I stumbled across a job at Wellbeing and decided to take a chance on it. I'm so glad that I did! It gave me the opportunity to grow both personally and professionally.'

'I loved being a hairdresser but moving to Wellbeing Teams is the best decision I made – I can work around my young son and feel good about being a working mum.'

'The experience I have gained has given me the confidence to go back to University to get a degree in Health & Social Care.'

'I thought my diagnosis of rheumatoid arthritis would rule me out of a career in care, but they helped me to realise that your life doesn't have to feel like it's over because of your condition and I love my job.'

(Source: team members)

Learning points

- Relational care challenges existing notions of professional boundaries; Wellbeing Team members talk about love and making someone's day
- To facilitate relational care, team members need to be encouraged and supported to bring their whole self to work and share hobbies and interests with people. Wellbeing Teams match team members, and people they support based on shared common interests wherever possible
- It is important to take a strengths-based approach: they explored 'gifts of the head, heart and hands' both of colleagues and people supported, to find opportunities for people to use and share their strengths
- Recruitment for values is key: skills can be taught but team numbers must have the heart for Wellbeing work. Innovative values-based workshops rather than interviews have enabled the right type of recruitment. These included assessing how people brought their whole self to work; gave feedback to each other; reflected, listened and worked together
- Innovation and creativity are needed to develop the environmental factors for relational care: self-management brings decision-making as close to people as possible and gives opportunities for this
- Paying attention to relationships applies equally to team members as to those supported, with workplaces that focus on social support and autonomy.

Wellbeing Teams instigated strategies to promote good relationships between team members, and deal with conflict, for example, communication
skills training and weekly tactical meetings

Buurtzorg Teams

The nature of the scheme

The Buurtzorg concept (meaning 'neighbourhood' and 'care') was developed in
the Netherlands in 2006 as a model of personal, social and clinical care delivery
by small, non-hierarchical nursing teams working on the basis of as few as possible different people serving each client and building relationships of trust. It is
this model that in part inspired the community-based projects described in the
sections above.

In 2017 a Buurtzorg test-and-learn initiative was agreed in West Suffolk, with
the intention of integrating health and social care provision for adults needing
care and support in their own homes. The aim was to address the problems
of confidence and continuity of relationships that arise when people who require care at home are often seen by multiple staff members on a given day and
possibly never see the same care worker or nurse again. The project had four
cross-disciplinary stakeholders: Suffolk County Council, West Suffolk Clinical Commissioning Group, West Suffolk NHS Foundation Trust and the West
Suffolk district councils.

What the Buurtzorg Model looks like

Buurtzorg teams have no hierarchy, make their own clinical and operational decisions and work in a specific neighbourhood. In contrast to the usual 'divided'
nature of health and social care, both are brought together under the umbrella
of one team. In this respect, the model goes a step further than Neighbourhood
Cares, where clients were not provided directly with clinical care by the team.
Because UK systems are well established into silos of health and social care, implementing Buurtzorg here presents a particular challenge.

Insofar as representing a model for nurturing relational care, Buurtzorg
clearly has the potential to do so, given that developing long-term personal
knowledge and trust between patient and nurse is at the heart of its ethos.
Whether the concept can achieve this objective in the UK or whether its value
is in inspiring and being adapted to 'home-grown' models that can be more
quickly embedded in the existing infrastructure remains a critical question.
Most evaluations conclude that this person-centred, relationship-based element of the model actually translates well to the UK but that the 'holistic'
element is somewhat more challenging.

Impacts

The main impact of the Suffolk project has been to indicate its role and value as a basis for new models. An evaluation was undertaken by the King's Fund in 2019, and they concluded that the

> West Suffolk system leaders involved in the project recognise that some of the core principles of self-managed or self-directed teams, delivering health and care within a framework of trusted assessment and working with local communities are excellent foundations of practice for our locality teams and should be protected into the future development following the 'test and learn' but that the purist model is more suited to the Dutch healthcare system and is difficult to introduce into a different system that is rapidly building its own integrated working partnerships.
>
> *(A review of the West Suffolk Buurtzorg test-and-learn in 2017–2018,*
> *Kings Fund, April 2019)*

This comment refers only to this particular project and does not fully reflect other more positive UK experience; there were factors in West Suffolk that were challenging in terms of the self-management aspect.

Learning points

The main learning points from the West Suffolk project are of interest but may not reflect the learning from other UK pilots. They can be summarised as follows:

* Rather than transferring the model wholesale into a new setting, consider what aspects will help achieve the desired aims and how these can be most easily implemented
* Devolving decision-making to the team requires infrastructure such as test location, IT systems to be put in place first, so that the team is not delayed in actually getting client provision under way
* Allow for extensive support and time for the team to develop and practise a shared understanding, as they are unlikely to be used to working in a non-hierarchical way: at least one year is needed for colleagues to grow trust and confidence in each other and the new model
* Build in learning 'breaks' so that the team is not under so much pressure to perform and deliver that there is no time to reflect and develop

Local community engagement and the tanteLouise initiative

Staying embedded in the local community is one of the key environmental factors for relational care, and the benefits and impacts of doing this were expressed by interviewees from the UK projects and homes.

THE LOCAL COMMUNITY: SUPPORT AND CONTINUITY

'I think it's important to keep old friends and keep in contact. I like to know what's going on where I used to live' (resident).

'There are people here who I knew; we all grew up in the same village. And I knew the grandparents of people who work here' (resident).

'Are the staff people who live locally?' 'Yes, all of them' (interviewer/owner).

'One lady goes to the local library for a reminiscing session; we're hoping to make that a group session, and ask in local schools' (owner).

'A lot of our residents go out into the town, and we want to bring the community into the care home. Most of our residents come from local families' (manager).

'A lot of them [the residents] are local; they used to know each other in school, in jobs. Some visitors here pop off and see other residents' (manager).

'Since you moved in do you keep in touch with friends and relatives?'

'Relatives, yes.'

'People in the town you used to know?'

'Yes, they pop in to see me. But we're all getting to the same age' (interviewer/resident).

'I'm keen for our lifestyle leads to leave the building and walk round, see what's there and say hello to people, offer to share facilities' (regional manager).

The nature of the tanteLouise scheme

TanteLouise is a Dutch care provider with 18 locations in the Netherlands. It prides itself on new ways of thinking grounded in a tradition of warm, loving care. It has taken a fresh approach to mitigating the worst effects of dementia, through a new scheme based on interactive learning, innovative technology and a determination to give older people as much freedom and autonomy as possible. The driving motivation is a dream to restore to them vitality and a meaningful life and significantly diminish frustration.

In 2014 the company started using technology to give its residents more freedom of movement, and in 2018 it opened a purpose-built open village in Hof van Nassau designed to give the maximum amount of freedom without compromising basic safety. One of its critical enablers is its links with a local dementia-friendly community.

What the village looks like

The development is home to 120 people in 15 houses (each with eight residents); there is a communal garden and a restaurant as well as other everyday services such as a small shop, a hairdressing salon and a laundry in which residents are allowed to volunteer, if they would like to. Residents can move around into areas outside their own house and have certain free ranges of movement depending on the presence of unseen (and non-frustrating) perimeters. There are divisions of freedom between the houses, between the inner area and the restaurant and between the entire village and the local community. These perimeters are controlled by the residents' wearables (similar to watches) that can be set according to the person's capacity and stage of dementia and that can be adjusted day by day, allowing them to go to appropriate areas but no further. They are linked to Bluetooth (inside the facility) and GPS (in the 'outside world') tracking systems, and control smart locks are installed on gates in the perimeters.

Freedom to go into the 'outside world' is enabled by the essential commitment of the local community, which in this case joined in a community-led project to make the surrounding area 'dementia friendly'. TanteLouise achieved this by working with their local principality (local authority), charities, local businesses and local residents.

Impacts

For residents:

- Quality of life significantly improved
- Greater mobility and independence
- Awareness levels higher
- Frustration levels reduced
- 90% reduction of sedative medication
- Continue to live in the 'here and now' rather than continually living in the past
- Re-learning takes place and loss of memory is less progressive

For staff:

- Residents more tranquil (and better able to relate)
- More rewarding relationships and job satisfaction
- Lower physical workload
- Fewer wheelchairs or bedridden patients

For the organisation:

- Enhanced reputation for quality care
- Maintain position as market leader and pioneer by operating as test bed for cutting-edge innovations and new approaches
- Reduction in costs for day-to-day background activities to focus on value-added services for residents
- Opportunity to share knowledge and best practice in health care at national and international level

Science and research enabling relational care and community engagement

TanteLouise uses a method called error-free learning, which works on the scientifically proven premise that people with dementia can still continue to learn (this is also the principle on which Montessori care discussed in Chapter 4 is based). Automatic forms of learning remain intact for a relatively long time, so error-free learning succeeds by focusing on activities that are done correctly, reinforced by a sense of positivity and achievement. Along with this approach, tanteLouise has created a new role called the Active Ageing Nurse, trained by psychologists in how to apply the method and assess the correct degree of freedom for each resident on a daily basis using a scoring model to help with decision making and provide guidance for interventions.

Technologies are used as part of the method in the form of a wearable for the resident and a tablet or smartphone for the nurse: the purpose of the technology is to support the method rather than dominate it. The use of augmented reality during the administration of medication has greatly reduced errors and saves staff time, which is released to enable staff to spend more time forming relationships with residents and 'smart glasses' can be worn by carers to enable a remote specialist to assess a situation while the actual care can be given by someone familiar to and trusted by the resident.

Because 'We think about possibilities rather than obstacles' (tanteLouise CEO) residents are enabled to regain as much autonomy as possible and to interact with a supportive local community based on realistic rather than worst-case risk assessment. 'The risks of restoring freedoms can be overestimated' (tanteLouise CEO).

Learning points

- New ways of working can improve life for everybody if everyone is involved in the design, testing and assessment of the initiative
- Assumptions and expectations about what older people can and cannot do, even those with advanced conditions, can be overcome
- Technology can be a positive force if used to support a new approach rather than being the primary rationale or driver for the approach
- The vision for new ways of working needs to be communicated to and shared by everyone involved
- Organisation change takes courage and ambition
- If everyone stays the same and keeps doing the same, then nothing will change

The potential for relational care in the community

There are many more examples around the country of localised projects where multidisciplinary teams save costs and improve health, such as the Flintshire Support Team linked to the Rapid Response and Rehabilitation team. 'As a result of the project there was a 31 per cent reduction in admissions to secondary care over a nine-month period ... with a possible saving of over £33,000 in acute hospital care' (Help the Aged, 2007, p. 117).

Gawande describes a University of Minnesota project, whereby two cohorts of older people were assigned between care by regular medical teams and care exclusively from a geriatric team, the latter providing care such as simplifying medications and monitoring good nutrition. Death rates in both groups were the same, but the patients of the geriatric team were 'a quarter less likely to become disabled and half as likely to develop depression' (2014, p. 44).

Older people, in common with other age groups, also choose to come together in community settings such as clubs, learning groups, University of the Third Age that can be very supportive and – without necessarily intending it – save the public purse considerable outlay by offering friendship, learning, activity and a sense of purpose. The list of options offered in a local library or online would be very long, and in a larger town or city, hundreds of such voluntary organisations usually exist, many run by older people. A team like Neighbourhood Cares will connect its clients into them.

Finally, often just at the point before a care home becomes unavoidable, there may well be the stage of hospitalisation. While the presence of the NHS means that we are fortunate to have access to (generally) very good hospitals regardless of our assets, and while medical staff are (nearly always) caring and compassionate, hospitals are not designed as places where relational care can easily be fostered: they are designed to deal with vital health needs and crises and are orientated towards cure and despatch. So when they become a longer-term 'home' for older people who need to move on, the situation is unsatisfactory and can lead to a great deal of discontent and lack of feeling settled. In one interview the manager of a care home group suggested, 'There should be more partnerships between hospitals and care home providers, so the homes can act as rehabilitators or step-down partners – this seems to make sense and would help with bed blocking.'

Provided that care at home, a care home or a nursing home place is available, the older person will rightly be moved on when it is safe. The problem arises when there is a desperate scramble to put care in place for the discharge. As the next chapter describes, the results of this can be damaging to the next phase of life. Staying in one's own home is idealised as 'a haven from the outside world...a place of love, unity and caring' (Cluff and Binstock, p.157), but as they point out the realities of providing care, there 'are often in conflict with the warm and comforting images' (ibid., p. 118). If planning for a departure from hospital is based on this idealisation, because no-one wished to think about it before the older person became acutely ill, then the resulting transition may not be a happy one. One of the benefits of care in the community by multidisciplinary teams is that they form settled and trusted relationships so that they can encourage this type of planning, they have the information required and, when the time comes, they can act as an independent friend in assisting with choices.

In conclusion, the type of community-based care described here offers models that have been proven to provide the benefits of relational care. Its impacts on older people and the wider community can be very significant; its effects are clearly felt by everyone whose lives have been improved and whose voices have been shared in this chapter.

Some further reading relating to this chapter

Loneliness

Evidence Review: Loneliness in Later Life (Davidson and Rossall, 2015, AgeUK)

Wellbeing Teams

https://wellbeingteams.org

Buurtzorg teams

Buurtzorg Briefing Document (Martin, 2015, Buurtzorg Britain & Ireland)

TanteLouise

A video about living in Hof van Nassau can be found at https://www.youtube.com/watch?v=xHEU2C5DfvE&feature=youtu.be

Alms Houses

The Alms Houses Association https://www.almshouses.org

Older people living in the community

As Time Goes By: Thoughts on Wellbeing in Later Years is a booklet based on the reflections of five older researchers who interviewed for the research report Wellbeing in Old Age (Ward et al., 2012). The booklet can be found on https://www.brighton.ac.uk/ssparc/research-projects/older-people-wellbeing-and-participation.aspx

3

INNOVATIONS IN LIVING TOGETHER

Relational care in residential settings

Living in residential settings

Innovation, together with an element of courage in terms of investment and commitment, can transform the provision of care to older people in their own homes from a ragged patchwork of rushed visits and ever-changing disempowered staff to a consistent, relationship-based support system that helps social workers, carers and clients feel valued. There comes a time when even the best community-based provision is no longer sufficient, however, and when residential schemes or homes providing personal or nursing care become essential.

It is more than unfortunate that care homes as a group often get bad press. It has already been noted that the Victorian workhouse casts a long shadow more than a century later, and this is exacerbated by grim but sadly true news stories about abuse, neglect and sudden closures. Older readers may remember the 1960s sitcom *Steptoe and Son*, and old Albert's fear of being 'put in a home'. With the more modern emphasis on staying independent, this fear still exists, now with an added helping of guilt about becoming a 'burden'. The question of what constitutes 'dependence' together with other assumptions and policies means that residential provision of various types needs fresh consideration in the light of the success of good relational care.

In this chapter, the issues of dependence, policy and transition will first be addressed; the key criteria for relational care will then be reviewed in the context of residential communities and through the voices of all those involved; and finally examples of innovations in shared living that enable the key criteria – and hence much happier places – will be presented.

Current policies affecting residential care

An aversion to the idea of 'dependence' has become endemic, and much policy is based on the aim of preventing such an apparently disastrous state and rescuing those at risk of it for as long as possible. As we will see later when looking at what independence and more importantly 'interdependence' really mean, this aversion arises from a number of causes and skews decision making.

Having one's own home and staying in it with the independence to organise one's life without reference to others sounds like a human right. But very few people are actually in this position, as the more likely scenario is continual negotiation and compromise with partner, other family members or house-mates; restrictions of income and choice; and landlords, mortgage lenders and other agencies. Nevertheless, while in one's own home, there is still choice over many matters of daily living, and older people rightly fear losing this control. Gawande tells the story of how Keren Brown Wilson came to develop the assisted living concept in response to this fear:

> The key word in her [mother's] mind was *home*. Home is the one place where your own priorities hold sway. At home, you decide how you spend your time, how you share your space, and how you manage your possessions.
>
> *(2014, p. 89)*

This fear, however, should not and cannot imply a denial of interconnectedness, and Wilson's response to her mother's distress in fact led to a concept based on healthy relationships.

The dominance of maintaining independence, in the minds of individuals planning for their future and in policy, can lead to unintended consequences. Barnes et al. talk of 'The Autonomy Myth', a phrase coined by Martha Fineman, and how it has impacted 'policy discourse and practices', quoting Sevenhuijsen: 'dependency appears as something that has to be overcome (citizens have to be made independent)' (2018, p. 27). Barnes et al. challenge the currently prevalent narrow interpretations of 'independence'. 'Dominant conceptualisations of autonomy, choice and control are evident not only in statutory policy...but are reflected in [some third sector] policies and guidelines' (ibid., p. 35).

VIEWS OF INDEPENDENCE

'One of the hardest things at the beginning was losing my independence. I've always been a sociable person, without having to be thrown together' (resident).

'I arranged a dental appointment for myself, apparently they [the home] should have known about it. It made me feel I'm losing my independence. I'm angry, I'm annoyed about it, and I know they are too' (resident).

'Our aim here is to promote independence' (owner).

'Over the years we have learnt that we don't necessarily have to do something because they are paying us. We have realised that independence is above everything else. It's all about feeling and wellbeing, not just that you are being taken care of' (owner/director).

These observations are not intended to lightly dismiss the high levels of physical and cognitive dependency now being seen in care homes. *My Home Life* notes that a 2006 survey indicated '82% are confused, forgetful, depressed or agitated... nearly half of residents are both immobile and incontinent' (Help the Aged, 2007, p. 96). The purpose is, rather, to question whether some policies may exacerbate these problems, and which can be ameliorated by good relational care.

There are other policies that affect the nature of care homes, which are addressed largely in the final chapter. These include funding policies, which in particular have influenced the shift from public to private provision noted in Chapter 1, and hence the nature of employment in care homes. An estimate of carers and managers – '72,000 employed by the local authority and 390,000 in the independent sector (private and voluntary)' (ibid., p. 130) – was made in 2004 and will almost certainly have moved further towards a higher proportion in private employment, which can be less secure.

The shift to non-Local Authority (LA) ownership, as well as funding policies, may also influence the allocation of older people into homes that are not located in their own community if these are cheaper for the LA or are the ones with an immediate vacancy. Yet maintaining links with their community, with friends, clubs, churches and so on, as well as with any local family, is important to wellbeing and to feeling more settled in the care home: 'The history of the home influences the way friendships are developed. If the resident population is local where friendships may have been in existence long before moving into the home ... friendships are conducted in a different way' (Mowat, 2014, p. 18).

Relational care in dementia specialist homes

The Office of National Statistics estimates that 850,000 people in the UK have dementia, but only around two thirds have been diagnosed; by 2025 it is forecast that one million people in the UK could be living with dementia, and by 2050 this could exceed two million (Living longer: how our population is changing, ONS, August 2018). Dementia UK reports that 311,730 people with dementia are living in care homes, 57.9% in residential care homes and 42.1% in nursing homes (Prince et al. (2014) Dementia UK: Update Second Edition), and the prevalence of dementia in care homes has risen from 56% in 2002 to 70% in 2013 *(A two-decade comparison of prevalence on behalf of the Medical Research Council,* Matthews et al., 2013).

Behind these statistics lies a complex picture of various stages of dementia – ranging from not formally recognised to the most advanced – and an equal complexity of funding levels and issues, with either or both LA and NHS funding, private payments and top-ups. Although these will be considered later, because they affect the resources available, fortunately the complicated scenario can to a large extent be set to one side when considering the creation of relational care environments. In some personal care, and most nursing care homes, residents can be assumed to have some reduced cognitive or physical function, and often there will be co-morbidity. This does not render them any less likely to benefit from relational care. Perhaps more importantly, it does not greatly affect the nature of optimum practices for providing it.

My work in homes where all or some residents had dementia led me to wonder whether, given that residents are living in different and changing realities, they would be able to form supportive relationships. But observation and discussion with them indicated that

> the very fact of having companionship available can be a great positive to many residents: people say things such as 'The company's nice, people are nice' and 'Just people walking around [make it] interesting.' Episodes of frustration or unhappiness that residents describe seem to be counterbalanced by company; when they speak of people being around, their demeanour can be seen to improve.
>
> *(Developing a Relational Model of Care, Woodward and Kartupelis, p. 96)*

The main difference is, that

> the demands on staff time are likely to be significantly greater… due to the different mode of listening required, the need to actively facilitate relationships, the slower pace of providing care in tune with residents and the more proactive role in liaising with families.
>
> *(Ibid., p. 116)*

Nevertheless, the bonds of care and friendship can form when the environment is right, as one interviewee said to me: 'the bond that is created between the staff and the residents here, and also the residents with other residents – that's the key' (ibid., p. 101).

Barnes et al. relate the effects of a study by Brannelly applying care ethics to working with people with dementia, which concluded that 'basing practices on the dialogical methodologies implied by care ethics offers a more effective approach to enabling participation from both the person with dementia and their families than practices starting from more individualised ideas of citizenship' (2018, p. 38).

There seems to be no reason to discount the value of relational care where people with dementia and their carers are concerned. Some pointers to resources about issues applying to dementia can be found in Appendix B.

Transition into residential care

The reluctant community

Moving into a new living environment is inevitably stressful, as anyone who has ever moved house will affirm. For the older person, the situation can be made more difficult if the move is hasty or forced – perhaps because they have been hospitalised and judged unlikely to regain full capacity to live alone again, or family and other carers feel that the situation has reached a point where they can no longer cope or their loved one is no longer safe alone.

Regardless of the reason, it must be accepted that the majority of older people have strong reservations about a move and that the care home often comprises 'a reluctant community… For the most part people would not choose to live in a care home and be surrounded by strangers' (Mowat, 2014, p. 32). This reluctance is natural given the great emotional significance of one's own home that 'embodies aspects of both current and former identities' (Barnes et al., 2018, p. 137), but it may also be based on known examples of poor care and the negative perceptions conveyed by media and discomfort with one's own ageing. 'Retirees are vexing and frustrating challenges to the model of adulthood that society holds dear', as Koch says (2000, p. 1).

Timing and preparation

Reluctance to accept the need for a different lifestyle, the desperate belief in independence as an unfettered good or an accident that brings matters to a crisis – whichever of these may be the cause, one of the key problems that makes transition more difficult is lack of time to work through the process and consequently the often-enforced lack of preparation. Managers of homes often refer to this issue: that the more rushed and the later in life the transition takes place, the more frail the older person is, and the harder it becomes to have the will and capacity to form new relationships.

Families can be an influence in this respect. '[Family] caregivers may continue to care for an elderly parent even when the physical and emotional care needs of the recipient indicate that institutional placement would benefit the individual and the family' (Cluff and Binstock, 2001, p. 164). Their source ascribes this to the children still seeking parental approval, but there could be many reasons why families continue to 'hang on'. Meanwhile, the family home becomes a burden, as while it 'can reinforce a sense of "ownership" and identity … it is also a physical entity that requires cleaning, maintenance and repair, and can thus be a source of anxiety' (Barnes et al., 2018, p. 95).

'There are no good ways of mitigating transition without careful long-term planning, which is expensive and not everyone is willing or able to do' (regional manager during interview). Knowledge is power, and if older people and their families start to talk about a move before crisis point is reached, they have time to explore options and consider what might work for them. 'The transition for residents and relatives can be eased if pressure on them is minimised; if they have access to all relevant information and … are able to maintain ownership of decisions about the future' (Help the Aged, 2007, p. 157). If at all possible, they should allow time to try out the home by visiting for lunches or a short stay, and social workers will encourage this if they are involved. Some homes have day centres for the local community, which is an ideal bridge.

Another issue is that anyone leaving hospital will get a six-week free re-habilitation care package, but because this is paid for by the state, the care provided will come from one of their appointed agencies, which is unlikely to be the provider that the older person may have been using, so relationships will be put on hold at a critical time. After this the older person may stay with the second team or return to the original one, but in any case, continuity will have been lost.

These points are important in the context of relational care, as the smoother the transition, the better it is timed, and the more control an older person has over the choices and decisions, the more likely it is that they will be in a frame of mind to look for benefits when moving and to have planned for the disbenefits, so that they can take advantage of the environmental factors favouring feelings of security and companionship.

DON'T LEAVE IT TOO LATE

'People are starved of contact at the end of life when they need it most. There should be better transition planning. When we know someone is deteriorat-ing, why not bring them in for a while so they get used to the environment and are ready to transition?' (carer).

'We are trying to keep people in their own home for longer so when they come into care their dependency is higher' (regional manager).

'They come into the care service at a very late stage, so that's short-lived and they have to transition into a nursing service. Then the NHS say they can't fund it, the LA can't fund it, the processes take longer and so cost more' (owner).

'Some come to us and pass away very quickly; there's no time for relation-ships to form' (manager).

'When new people come in, you talk to them and soon know them'. 'Yes, but many are in the late stages of illness and the amount who can sit and talk together is unfortunately very limited' (two residents in conversation).

'Nowadays they come into us when they're much more frail in their de-mentia, whereas they used to come in the early stages. Families keep them at home until they reach crisis point' (office manager).

'Frailty affects how easily people settle in, especially if they're bed bound' (activities co-ordinator).

'It works better when it's not at point of crisis someone has to go into care' (regional manager).

Amelioration

My Home Life quotes from a study by Kelleher that underlines the importance of getting it right first time: 'I didn't make any decision about coming here. I was forced here. My flat was sold and then it all went haywire… For me it will never work out' (2007, p. 47). It need not be like that if there is time to plan, and the quote above is followed by a contrasting one: 'I made the decision myself. I decided to make it my home…I'm pleased – I'm proud. I've done this for myself.'

Even if such complete control is not possible, if a person is resilient they will be more able to adapt and embrace the new experience, acknowledging 'the importance of moving from "outsider" to "insider"' (Barnes et al., 2018, p. 139). Recognising and addressing fears is better done with the support of others and can bring the empowerment of making one's own choices in shaping a residential environment and progressing towards forming new bonds. 'Relationships with their immediate environment as well as with other people … are important in sustaining identities in new circumstances' (ibid.)

During and after a move, the role of the family is a complex one and has the potential to be negative or positive.

> Many relatives are able to establish a new role in the life of the older person within their new environment … Once older people are settled within care homes, family care-givers have been identified as a resource on a number of levels (Hertzberg and Ekman 2003).
>
> *(Help the Aged, 2007, p. 70)*

Relatives may well also become and stay as formal or informal volunteers in the home, if they are helped to feel part of its community.

GETTING TRANSITION RIGHT

'I absolutely wish people moved in sooner, not everybody has a positive experience out in the community. But we have to focus on the here and now, and how we can make a difference going forward' (manager).

'We can do that [give a taster] in the lead up if possible, but sometimes it's an emergency situation and that can't be done' (regional manager).

'If people come in from the community with their loved ones, perhaps for tea and cake, then when the time comes they move into the home better as a result' (carer).

'[Coming in here] was obvious; my husband had died and there was nothing left for me at home' (resident).

'My husband had dementia, and my sons said, "You're not managing", and within three days we were in here. It was difficult at first but I was pleased' (resident who had moved in as a couple).

Friends, family, community and the care home can all be allies in finding the resilience to make a timely move. The tyrannies of inflexibility and independence can both impede it. Inflexibility can turn a well-meaning care home into a prison, if everything that makes life worthwhile becomes forbidden on health and safety grounds and will deter older people from making a move. According to the Eden Alternative programme (2013), 'the three main plagues affecting older people living in care homes are loneliness, helplessness and boredom'. Fortunately, there are excellent examples of how this has been addressed by lateral thinking in exemplary homes, referred to in following chapters. Nevertheless, as far as independence is concerned, there is a need for societal change.

Revisiting independence

In 1943 Abraham Maslow published his famous 'Theory of Human Motivation' and proposed the concept of a hierarchy of human needs. Once those basic to survival have been met, our next most important needs are for love and belonging. These are surely incompatible with total independence, and moreover as Gawande notes, people are willing to forego basic survival needs 'for the sake of something beyond themselves' (2014, p. 93). If no-one is ever truly independent, then why is the concept so powerful and mesmerising? Why can we not accept that interdependence is the true human state from the day we are born small and powerless to the day we die, holding a beloved hand if we are fortunate?

Perhaps it is because autonomy and freedom (of choice, spirit, mind) are so easily confused with independence, while they are actually quite different. Our more religious forebears may have had less difficulty with this; as Mowat and Mowat say, 'Our actual control over our lives is always precarious and often an illusion'. They suggest we relinquish control to God's love, although 'our culture has emphasised increasingly our need to be independent' (2018, p. 48). Those who are non-religious need not reject the conclusion of this assertion, even if they do not agree with the proposal, but might instead be prompted to redefine independence, acknowledging that 'We can never be truly autonomous individuals for we each need others at some point in our lives. We are in reality interdependent, we need community' (MacKinlay in Jewell, 2004, p. 79).

Another reason to re-assess the value of independence is that it may not be chosen but instead may be imposed by circumstance or assumed norms. Barnes et al. record an interview with an older lady describing this situation: 'She asserted her independence, but this was not because she valued independence in its own right, but because she had learnt not to expect help' (2018, p. 119).

Even those who do not wish to redefine the idea of independence might accept that living alone can actually erode independence, if it engenders poor eating, unmonitored falls, forgotten medication and so on, leading to greater frailty and perhaps hospitalisation. They may also agree that the right residential home can be preferable to 'care at home' if the latter involves reduced autonomy for the older person – 'the physical environment of a private home can actually impede an individual's performance of the activities of daily living' (Cluff and Binstock, p. 162) – or means that other family members must sacrifice their normal lives: 'The introduction of high-tech care into the home also poses special physical and emotional challenges … to the family' (ibid., p. 163).

AUTONOMY AND FREEDOM

'We as a society are trying to keep people in their own homes for longer, so when they come into care their dependency is higher' (owner).

'I've still got my marbles and am perfectly capable of doing things' (resident).

'Do you feel you have lost your independence?'

'At this stage of one's life, when you can't do the things for yourself you used to, it's wonderful. Everything is done for you, the bed is made, the room is clean, food is put on the table' (interviewer/resident).

"Maybe people can't manage the maintenance or the garden, and they want the reassurance of someone being around, but they don't want to lose everything they've been able to do. It needs a change of mindset, not fear of going into 'one of those places'" (regional manager).

Relational care in residential settings

When you visit a care home, are you being welcomed into someone's family abode or entering an institution? Are the older people you meet there apathetic or distressed or living very much as they would at 'home'? Perhaps their lives are more filled and fulfilled than if they were still in their original family home? Are the staff stressed or detached or do they pause for a friendly word? All these are possible scenarios, influenced by resources, decisions made by owners, managers, staff and of course by residents themselves. There are many reasons why a home might be a miserable, restricted place, but there is no good reason for it to be so.

There are also many reasons why it could be somewhere that nurtures joy and life, accepts sadness and bereavement, helps people through change and fragility. Chapter 1 addressed the important role that relational care can play in supporting better lives and outcomes – 'practices that recognise the relational and contextual rather than rational dimensions of older people's lives are more likely to enable positive experiences' (Barnes et al., 2018, p. 35) – and proposed that the key criteria of relational care include a sense of: being known, accepted and loved; feeling safe and secure; having as much autonomy as possible and being enabled to contribute; and re-creation of family or community. The environmental factors that promote these senses were illustrated in Chapter 1 and will be reviewed below.

Gawande describes his grandmother-in-law's desire to 'remain in charge of her life' and his father-in-law's search for a 'place she would like and thrive in', but although they found what appeared to be the right place, with activities and pleasant individual accommodation, she did not thrive and was quietly unhappy. She said, '"It just isn't home." To [her it] was a mere facsimile of home. And having a place that genuinely feels like your home can seem as essential to a person as water to a fish' (2014, pp. 59 and 66). So what does make a home?

Listening to over 100 people in 40 different homes for the original Abbeyfield Society study described in detail in *Developing a Relational Model of Care* (Woodward and Kartupelis, 2018), and another 50 people in 13 different locations since, what they say about these factors is more revealing than any second-hand description. For the second study that has informed this book, I visited and spent time in a wide variety of homes in city and rural settings, in the South, North, Midlands, Yorkshire regions and London, owned by the Abbeyfield Society, Anchor Hanover, Hallmark and Milford Care Homes groups, as well as independents such as Glenfields, Nightingale House and Wren Hall. They were chosen mainly on the recommendation of leading reformers and campaigners in the ageing care sector, as well as on my previous knowledge, as exhibiting good relational practice and innovation.

Before considering how the positive environmental factors found in these homes can be established in other existing and new homes, a reminder of what the lived reality feels like and why it matters can be heard in some more quotes from interviewees.

RELATIONSHIPS, LOVE AND AFFECTION

'We talk about whether we can say "love" and hug people, there's a CQC thing about being too tactile, but we do it here and in most of our homes' (regional manager).

'I have residents who I address as Mrs or Mr and some as Duck or Lovey. It depends on the person. If I went to one of them and said, "Good Morning Mrs Smith", it would throw her; the first thing we do is hug' (care assistant).

'There's more hugs in this home, kisses, linking arms, holding hands, banter...' (manager).

'You can't buy happiness and love. There's no price on it' (carer).

'It's a loved place and I love working here' (activities manager).

'You have to care; you find yourself getting quite passionate' (office manager).

'We're a small home and I think we have excellent relationships; it's mainly about time. We spend quite a bit of time with our residents and their families. I wish we could afford more staff' (owner).

Belonging

'Some [residents] talk about personal things; they trust you enough to confide. Some residents take an interest [in the team] as people. We're friends I think' (care assistant).

'The carers are like family. We know all about them, their children' (group of residents).

'I need to learn to be kind and gentle like her [referring to one of the residents]. I like to spend time talking to her' (carer).

'Food and shelter may be the basics, but then we start talking about relationships, feeling secure, our sense of belonging. That's the real stuff we should be providing' (manager).

'They build a bond which is stronger than just a clients' and workers' bond. The intimacy between a carer and resident – it goes beyond that' (owner/director).

Friendship

'We have some unique bonds here. There are three ladies who never leave each other's sides; they're creating and building their own friendships. If one has a family come in to take her out, they all go' (carer).

'Have you made friends here?'

'Yes, definitely. There are enough people to find something in common' (resident).

Creating family

'Everyone talks about it being like a family here?'

'Absolutely'

'So what would you say your role is?'

'Like siblings – there's a serious time and a messing-around time' (interviewer/carer).

'And I'm like Mum' (manager).

'It's like working with my family' (carer, sitting with group of residents and looking at them all when she said this).

'The carers are like family' (resident).

'Residents here are called family members; my husband is a farmer, but he comes in and helps and knows everyone' (office manager).

Making a contribution

'When you have no-one to make a cup of tea for, then life is over. If they [residents] can do something important for us in our lives, then that builds a better relationship' (carer).

'Our residents are key in making decisions about menus, about events, and how we run them' (manager).

'When we're clearing up at mealtimes, one lady tells us if we're not doing it right. She likes to look after us, wipe the tables' (care assistant).

'If someone is calling out, they [another resident] will go over and chat' (care assistant).

'The residents offer us support; we have a lot of banter' (manager).

'I often say, "Tell me how to do it [the gardening]". I'll let them tell me, and in that way they're still involved' (carer).

'We always encourage people to serve themselves and others if they wish' (carer).

Providing security

'Having consistent team members, so they can build that relationship, gives people the confidence to join in' (manager).

'Essential to have a dedicated team, rather than moving around, except when cover is needed' (deputy manager).

'The garden is a safe environment – it's tranquil' (resident).

'We want people to feel secure and comfortable, everything they need around them within easy reach' (manager).

'People should not have to leave – ever – if they don't want to' (care assistant).

Dignity, respect and trust

'I have some residents who don't like banter and like to be addressed in a certain manner. That's respect, isn't it? (carer).

'We ensure people keep their own clothes by doing individual washing. Bulk washing didn't work' (carer).

'We have a log of all a person's clothes, and we label them. Staff check people get the right things back' (carer).

'It's extremely important we get to know every individual, and tailor things to each individual' (owner).

Some of the environmental factors that promote these beneficial feelings are vividly described by those who experience them daily.

THE PHYSICAL ENVIRONMENT

'Even if it's only a little pot you loved and you couldn't take it with you, or a bookcase that didn't match with the style, you're grieving because you had to move out of your home and leave something important behind' (care worker).

'I like to chat, to look at pictures. There are quiet spaces, little areas' (resident).

'Some people walk in here and think, *God, all the colour!* But people with dementia need the more vibrant colours, otherwise everything is grey-looking' (owner/director).

'They watch TV as a group; we encourage it. For the tennis final they had strawberries and cream and a glass of wine' (manager).

Gardens and getting outdoors

'Some people just like to potter in the garden and do their own thing' (manager).

'All our lounges have direct access to outside. There are some enclosed terraces, but everyone can get to the main garden' (owner).

'What more would most want here? A big, big garden for the residents. We do have a good garden but not easy access – we're working on it' (manager).

'The one thing I wish is that we had more access to transport so I could take them out more. People want outings, but we're up against transport; we used to do it every week, but it lost a lot of funding [from the Local Authority]' (carer).

Sharing meals

'Lunch is at one o'clock but everyone can eat whenever they want as well' (manager).

'We have things like farmhouse kitchens, and in other dining rooms residents are choosing to put the tables together because they like a family feel' (director).

'The food is home cooked and people can choose what they want. It's what we were used to in ordinary life' (resident).

Challenges and costs of supporting relational care

Hearing how best practice feels in the lived environment might beg the questions, why doesn't everyone do it this way? And, does it cost a lot more to do it this way?

In answer to the first question, most organisations, public or private, have engrained ways of doing things that can be very hard to alter. They may not see any need to change or consider it too difficult and not worth the effort or be concerned about criticism from customers, users, shareholders, regulatory bodies and public opinion. No-one wants to get it wrong, and certainly no-one wants to compromise their organisation's value and reputation. In general, the larger the organisation, the harder it is to turn it around, as it will lack the agility of the smaller group or independent care home and will be answerable to more stakeholders. However, having lived beside the Thames, I have seen very large ships turned around by very small tugs!

There are inevitably costs associated with change, not necessarily just financial ones. In the next chapter, we will look at instituting major changes in care practice. These need not be financially prohibitive but require new visions and adopting a very different outlook, yet as will be shown, most of the people involved have found the rewards greater than the challenges.

In this chapter, several approaches to introducing the factors for relational care will be presented: some involve making changes to existing care homes; others are new build developments incorporating the critical factors.

There may be financial costs relating to the physical 'bricks and mortar' changes, varying from thousands to millions of pounds, although of course the major spend of new build represents a long-term investment with calculated returns. There are also staff costs, mainly training and management support in introducing new practices, perhaps also increasing the staff to resident ratio in some cases. Savings in recruitment can significantly help to offset these.

Measurement of change where there are attitudinal as well as financial variables is not always easy, but there are a number of methodologies. Some of the more widely used are presented briefly in Appendix A, together with additional resources on measurement tools. The general dominance of measurement in the context of complex human judgements and the need to meet financial criteria without neglecting ethical ones are also considered in Chapter 6.

Reasons to support relational care

The voices of older people and care staff, and the way they describe their experiences in residential settings that nurture relational care, advocate powerfully for its benefits: enhanced life satisfaction, the needs to be loved, accepted and valued being met, feelings of security and not having to face the future alone.

There is also the question of meeting external criteria, in particular the Care Quality Commission evaluations, but these do not contradict the indicators for relational care, although they may not cover all the aspects.

The care sector is continually growing and developing, and the environmental factors that support the criteria for relational care must stay under review and adapt to the expectations of different generations. For example, shared meals are an important aspect, but many older people nowadays have not had the experience of eating regular family meals, especially if they have had a busy working life. Should this factor be abandoned when it is clearly so popular with interviewees, or can it be adapted to be more flexible but still give the benefits of companionship, good nutrition and discreet monitoring? This type of issue may mean tracking and adjusting different approaches and also trying out practices which need time to bed-in rather than immediately attempting to meet all residents' assumed needs at once.

The report *My Home Life* (Help the Aged, 2007) explores the impact of relational factors on wellbeing and optimum care. It cites Davies in *The Care Needs of Older People and Family Caregivers in Continuing Care Settings*:

> Davies describes three types of community within care homes for older people: the controlled community, the cosmetic community, and the complete community, arguing that the 'complete community' is consistent with the most positive experiences for older people and promotes 'best care'. In the 'complete community' objectives are enablement and partnership ... interdependence is an important value; and close links are made with the local community.
>
> *(p. 148)*

However, it assumes rather than evidences hard cost-savings.

Replicating new approaches to relational care in existing homes

Many of the environmental factors that support relational care can be introduced into existing care homes, and not all require any substantial physical changes; they are, however, likely to demand culture change and a policy based on recognition of the benefits of supporting and investing in meeting the key criteria. There are a number of successful practices that could be developed and adapted to a further level. Some can be quite small scale and incremental, while others may really need to be implemented from scratch.

One of the overarching purposes of changing to a more relational model is to encourage a greater sense of belonging and companionship, and the value of achieving this could be heard in many of the interviews in a variety of homes.

BELONGING TO THE 'FAMILY' OF THE HOME

'Residents, relatives and staff are one family – we are a family, we are dysfunctional, we fall out, [and] we make up' (manager).

'It's like a family here, I've picked up so much in a week from what people are telling me, even the residents talking about each other' (new carer).

'Some people don't have any family near; that's when staff become their adopted family, which is nice' (office manager).

'It's our family, and everyone is affected by what happens' (carer).

'We call ourselves a family, and sometimes people think it's a bit of a cliché but genuinely there is that level of affection between residents and team' (activities manager).

'This is a family and we [the staff] are its supporters – it's about enabling family life to continue within the homes' (carer and manager).

Some examples of more incremental but nevertheless impactful change are: creating smaller, more relationship-friendly areas and design; introducing whole-team involvement; encouraging family and volunteer engagement; changing recruitment practices; and developing policies that recognise the individual potential of each home to be more relational in its operation.

There are also factors that are easier to plan into new-build – addressed in the next section – but that are also possible to introduce into existing homes, such as dividing lounges and re-working garden spaces.

Re-purposing the physical environment

One of the key criteria for relational care is a model of living that enables people to be known to one another and build trust, and many interviewees described this model by reference to 'family'. Ensuring that a large home is divided into smaller groupings, but that movement between them is possible, favours this model. Wren Hall provides a good example of this. As the home got bigger, the 'family feel' started to get lost; their response was to divide the premises into four 'lounges', each with its own dining room, seating areas and all facilities to hand. Each lounge serves 16 residents with a team of four dedicated staff, encouraging 'being known' and forming stable relationships. Every lounge is distinctive and very much a 'home', with residents' possessions and artwork around, small groupings of chairs and an area for everyone to make a drink when they feel like it; however, people are not confined and can visit other lounges or meet in the garden, as all the lounges have direct access to the outside. As the director says, 'We've created an environment where people feel safe and comfortable and they have everything they need within easy reach.'

As I observed after visiting homes of many different sizes,

> the dynamics of family relationships seem to adapt to various models … In smaller homes, each person will of necessity be in some sort of relationship with every other person, leading to a higher level of understanding but potentially more serious problems if one person is 'difficult'… larger developments tend to act as mini-villages, with people viewing each other as neighbours, and the family bonds forming between those who identify with others.
>
> (Woodward and Kartupelis, 2018, p. 83)

Another key criterion is to have the capability of offering the choice of company and privacy throughout the day. Both this capability and the family model rely in part on the design and layout of communal rooms facilitating interaction and having quiet spaces, which means that a variety of small lounges is ideal, at least one of them without a TV. If this is impossible, then at least the only lounge should be arranged such that the TV is at one end, and dominating the space as little as possible, and there are small groupings of chairs and tables at the other; the chairs should be easily moveable.

HOW THE RIGHT DESIGN HELPS

'In some places, there's no atmosphere, no feeling. It's very cold' (manager).

'Most of our homes are split into small communities; you do end up having that family feel in each' (regional manager).

'It feels more like home now we've created smaller living areas' (owner).

'I notice you have a lot of small areas?' 'They're used to read sometimes. I've set the chairs so people can see each other, and have a conversation' (interviewer/manager).

'It's easy to talk in private. Some people will share difficult stuff' (residential care assistant).

'You could reproduce what we've done here, moved away from the hotel model, added a day centre and an end of life suite' (owner).

'This is a home from home, we have personal belongings around, and we watch discretely to make sure they're not moved away' (office manager).

'Some homes are five-star hotel style, and they're being sold to the family not the individual. I don't think anybody wants to go and live in a hotel for ever' (owner/director).

Insofar as meals are concerned, the kitchen is at the heart of the family, and

> A good architect will find ways of making the division required for safety purposes as 'permeable' as possible with the dining room, so that the cook can easily talk to residents and their appetite can be stimulated by the sights and smells of cooking.
>
> *(Ibid., p. 79)*

In some Hallmark homes, for example, the model of the 'farmhouse kitchen' enables this sort of interaction and could be replicable depending on cost and space. The dining room itself can be designed to encourage discussion, and for residents who wish to, to be able to help others. Managers said people particularly appreciated plenty of light, preferably daylight, and liked to have personal possessions around; this area is not a restaurant, but a family room. In the case of a larger development, it is ideal to have a restaurant-style or café-style facility as well, for visiting families.

Another idea that was very popular where it is possible is an old-fashioned cinema, perhaps seating up to a dozen people – there is an excellent example at Anchor Hanover's Silk Court in London. This was designed in consultation with residents (the Group aims for this input in all its homes), and with its eclectic 1950s look is used not only for films but also for residents to view, for example, a live-streamed family wedding. If a dominant TV in the lounge is an issue, the cinema could also be used as a TV room. Again, cost and space may be limiting factors, but imagination need not.

Some aspects of design may have to be balanced against risk, such as access to cooking facilities. This issue is addressed further in the section on the Montessori enabling approach in the next chapter, but it is worth noting that perceived risk can sometimes be overcome, opening the way for relationship-friendly design and activity.

WORKING AROUND RISK

'The caring staff sometimes feel a barrier with health and safety. They're worried – the teapot is too heavy, too hot. This creates a barrier to self-care. We talked to CQC; they say it's home specific' (owner).

'One lady wanted to brush the floor, and I asked why she wasn't allowed; the member of staff said, "Health and Safety", so I said, "That lady's been using a broom since before you were born probably." So I gave her the broom, and she did an amazing job; it's become her job every day, and she has a sense of purpose' (manager).

'Of course they can go to the shop or the pub. Why not? As long as they have the capacity, it's their decision' (manager).

'We do very well, cope with wheelchairs and things. We go to museums, the opera. We're very lucky' (resident).

'Everyone is entitled to take some risk; the residents would be in bubble wrap if it was up to Health and Safety. CQC want assessments, but they are very much about seeing residents lead a fulfilled life, so if we have assessed they're happy with that' (regional manager).

Gardens and outdoors

Access to outdoors and the ability to go out into the fresh air and local community (whether individually or in a group, assisted or on one's own) are highly valued by residents. Garden rooms and summerhouses were much prized by managers to whom I spoke, giving spaces for quiet contemplation and conversation and creating a bridge with the outside world. 'Gardens can play a range of roles in the life of a home: encourage mobility and exercise; provide a connection to nature; offer extra room and lift the spirits' (Woodward and Kartupelis, 2018, p. 53). If a home already has a garden, and fortunately many do, then a modest re-design can make a great difference. Ideas include statues, safe water features, easy-to-follow paths, fruit trees and of course summerhouses. Nest boxes give the pleasure of watching the renewal of life, and a topic of conversation, especially if they have a web cam that can be transmitted to a screen in a quiet communal area.

In 2017, The Abbeyfield Society developed a programme called 'A Breath of Fresh Air' with Dementia Adventure; although intended for people with dementia, the principles could apply more generally. They are based on encouraging outdoor activities, such as weekly garden walks and exercise classes as well as making the external space as accessible as possible, whether for sitting or getting involved in gardening. They developed a method of balancing potential risk against benefits. The benefits demonstrated by a pilot project were significant, including a major reduction in loneliness and improvement in mood, sleep and appetite and a decreased number of falls.

Outings may be ambitious – some homes I visited were planning trips to the seaside or even a weekend abroad – or they may be much more modest and assist with staying linked to the local community. Outings not only are enjoyable in themselves but also bring back good memories and build new ones for conversation over lunch or tea, encouraging the formation of relationships. They represent a hope for the future, something to look forward to and plan for. If at all possible, building trips out into the home's timetable adds to contentment and interaction.

GETTING OUTSIDE

'The gardens are nice, you can sit in the open'
'Is that important?'
'Very much so, being in the open, having a choice what to do' (resident/interviewer).
'Residents love the garden. They can take their breakfast outside in the summertime. It needs investment though' (manager).
'Gardens can be of great emotional significance' (manager).
'People love going on outings' (owner).

The support of families and volunteers

Encouraging the greater engagement of relatives in the life of the home should happen naturally but may need to become embedded in the ethos; it makes for more contentment and continuity for residents, is reassuring for relatives and can make the life of staff easier if they and the relatives feel they are 'on the same side'. Further, if the atmosphere is encouraging and friendly to them, visitors can get attached to the home themselves and become volunteers.

Volunteers are a great asset to a home, augmenting staff time, bringing in the 'outside', fostering connections with the local community and offering additional skills and interests. They may also be trustees if the home is owned by a charity. They can be found through residents' families and local connections such as clubs, colleges and churches. Unless they are coming in for a specific purpose, such as to give computer training, it is important that they make a commitment, as they are likely to form supportive relationships with staff and residents, which should be sustained and reliable.

The good practice described above is reflected in these voices.

FAMILIES AND THE 'FAMILY' OF THE HOME

'The relationships we build are with older people and their families' (project manager).

'Families are good at interacting with others when they come in' (manager).

'Some of the families have relationships with other residents as well, go and talk to them' (carer).

'Families tend to work in unison with each other and us; there are certain things they can tell us that help us do our job better' (office manager).

'My team support each other when residents pass away, and often you'll find the family consoling the carer' (team manager).

'We have to consider – if there's a lady living here whose husband comes in every day, there isn't much to talk about – could we involve them both in an activity?' (activities co-ordinator).

Whole-team involvement

A more radical but very successful change, in terms of fostering a network of relationships, is to review the approach to organising roles of staff and provision of activities. Rigid roles are not a good basis for creating a 'family' where everyone is known and valued; members of staff are not 'the cleaner' or 'the handyman'; although those are the jobs in which they are employed, they are people in their own right who are likely to be interested in others, if given the encouragement and trusted to get to know older people and other staff. This demands some flexibility about the timing of tasks and an appreciation that chatting and listening are not a waste of time. It also means understanding on the part of managers and owners that some chatting can happen during tasks, and sometimes it will be necessary to pause and give full attention to the other person; and that the time this takes, far from being wasted, is part of fulfilling the real purpose of the home.

BREAKING DOWN BARRIERS

'The handyman has tasks to do to keep the home safe, but that's nothing that can't wait ten minutes for that important chat to take place, to make a difference' (manager).

'Someone cleaning the room is engaging with the resident' (manager).

'We've done every job. We're part of all the teams. Doesn't matter what department you work in, the outcome is about the residents' (office and training manager).

'Site maintenance have become part of the family as well. Some places use external contractors who don't turn up for days' (owner).

> 'The whole home approach, it doesn't have to be a care team member [with a resident] (training manager).
> 'We all muck in, which creates a family feel' (owner/director).

Nearly all care homes have an activities programme, and re-visioning how this is delivered can be an excellent way of encouraging a whole team approach and getting everyone more engaged with one another. Anchor Hanover's 'Active' initiative is an example of a step change programme designed to promote a whole home approach to wellness and activities. By moving away from one person having responsibility for organising resident engagement and instead drawing in all colleagues, including housekeeping, maintenance and catering teams, Anchor Hanover has put wellness at the heart of its care homes. The basic principle is that the more that every colleague engages with residents and promotes wellbeing, the more opportunities there will be for meaningful occupation and shared hobbies and interests.

They have achieved this by removing the activity co-ordinator role and instead training wellness co-ordinators who help each home to become a community of shared ideas and activities. Key colleagues already working in the home are given time and training to develop new skills as 'champions' and to become fully involved themselves, in promoting and sharing interests from physical activity to art classes. To support the process, Anchor Hanover has invested corporately in new technology and equipment and also given each home an enhanced flexible budget. They report that not only do residents broaden their horizons but also are enabled to contribute to the life of the home: 'there are heart-warming examples… going horse riding every week, attending a gym fitness class, running a yoga class, delivering a reading club'.

Another great advantage to taking the whole team approach and recognising and encouraging engagement in this way is that it fosters mutual support within the team. This is a key factor in delivering successful relational care and is mentioned by many interviewees from various homes providing examples of best practice.

TEAM SUPPORT

'It's all about relationships, not just about supporting residents, but supporting team members as well' (owner/director).

'We have an employee assistance programme, but I don't think I know of anyone who has used it, because of the support network in the home. It's more personal, a lot easier to find comfort' (manager).

'Who do you first turn to in difficult situations?'

'Each other' (carers).

'We support each other as a team [when residents pass away]. We reminisce about the person. There is an organisation you can call, but it's better to get together and talk about the person' (manager).

'Who do you turn to when you feel down?'

'Managers, team leaders, they're all brilliant' (interviewer/co-ordinator).

'The staff are close; they do genuinely get on well. Problems are dealt with. If you're not going to care, you won't be here' (care worker).

'The team, we draw on each other for support. They are like our own family' (care worker).

'If the team are happy, it's much easier for them to make the residents and families happier' (activities co-ordinator).

Staffing and recruitment

All the factors that make for relational care are as beneficial to staff as residents: they work together to create an environment where people feel valued, trusted and settled. One way in which this can be achieved is by 'blending' the day-to-day tasks with conversation and affectionate touch, so that older people do not feel 'done to' as objects of concern but are partners in their own care and can give back through the human interaction with a known team. Good carers are highly skilled at doing this, understanding and responding to moods and needs, and their presence acts as an example to newer team members that caring is an ongoing mutual endeavour and not a task tick-list.

CARING AND CARE TASKS HAPPEN TOGETHER

'It was hard at the beginning to break that routine, task-oriented structure. But that doesn't provide emotional support to residents; it doesn't build relationships' (regional manager).

'In personal care, someone getting washed and dressed maybe, that should still be an enjoyable, interactive time' (carer).

'You have to start with the culture, move away from the task focus – if that bed doesn't get made in the next five minutes, it doesn't matter, if you've been doing the things that do matter and made a positive impact' (manager).

'They [carers] get time throughout a shift to spend with residents; we've built it into the rota' (owner).

'Staff like to join in; it brings them close to residents' (carer).

'Documentation is important, but we keep it in the office and try to spend as much time as possible with the residents' (administrator).

'We don't use an outside organisation; our own staff have been trained, are empowered to deliver, so if the residents say they want to do something, we can do it whenever they want, it's instant. It makes a massive difference' (regional manager).

'I'm a buddy – I join in completely' (care assistant).

'I've come from quite a big house and I'm really enjoying having a smaller group, spending more time with people' (care assistant).

'If you relied on Local Authority money, you couldn't have the ratio of staff to give them any time' (owner).

This attitude can be encouraged by a conscious change in ethos – should one be needed – underpinning practical changes such as new approaches to recruitment to select for 'heart' rather than qualifications, careful induction to reduce turnover and individual training programmes to help people develop and gain their qualifications as part of a personal support system. Similarly, staff should be valued through a fair and realistic level of pay and flexibility to meet their needs, given that flexibility is expected of them. The return on this investment is not only in meeting the ethical imperative of optimising life for residents and carers but also financial insofar as staff turnover can be reduced, recruitment and induction costs saved, and reputation enhanced.

It is interesting to look at how the relational home recruits staff who will fit with its ethos, what they look for and how they often involve residents in the process, and their comments on retention and long-term team stability.

RECRUITMENT

'[When we're recruiting] we have a set of questions and the residents ask them, they do the interview and ask their own questions as well. I sit back and write it all down' (manager).

'We've just had a big recruitment day. People think you need qualifications, but to be a carer you must have a heart' (carer).

'When interviewing don't pick people who see it as a job. Caring has to come from the heart' (office manager).

'We spend quite a lot of time with our residents; I think it's partly about who we employ, and the rigorous induction. You have to want to care; it's not just a job' (manager).

'We make judgements during an interview; we get used to spotting things that aren't right' (training manager).

'We use a psychometric test for job fit; we've identified what's most important: honesty, emotional conscientiousness' (owner).

'When we're recruiting, we think about diversity in the team, because for example some people need calm, some need energising. Every resident is different. But we always look for empathy and kindness' (owner/director).

Retention

'Our staff turnover is far less than average, and it's basically in the first four months after joining us. After that, they stick with us. I think that's our biggest saving – because staff stay with us' (owner).

'We nearly always promote from within' (owner).

'If staff go past six months, they'll stay a lot longer; we know that's the sticking point' (owner/director).

'When recruiting I try to match personality to which quarter of the home they will work in; then we rarely move them around' (deputy manager).

'There's a split between your biological and psychological families. I love my job but I also have small children. People need me here and people need me at home' (carer).

There is so much that can be done to make existing homes happier and more successful places – successful for residents, staff and owners. Each has its own potential and challenges; in some there are already good foundations and small changes will make a real difference, while others may give returns on investment in a more radical review.

Re-creating home and family models in new build and conversions

While so much can be done to adapt existing homes, their ethos, practice and layout, there are clearly limitations: in terms of staff who may not be comfortable with a new regime, and buildings which simply do not have the space for internal reconfiguration, or get planning permission and funding for extension. When a group decides on a new build, it has far more flexibility to incorporate relational design.

Following the extensive study with Abbeyfield, already described in Chapter 1 and above, the charity's Development department, working with an architect with considerable experience of care homes, drew up design guidelines to reflect the impact of the research on the built environment and its influence on emotional and spiritual as well as physical life. As the French philosopher and clergyman Ernest Dimnet said in *What We Live By* (1932), 'Architecture, of all the arts, is the one which acts the most slowly, but the most surely, on the soul'.

Good examples of how 'bricks and mortar' really do matter are to be found in The Abbeyfield Society's Hope Bank View independent living in Silksworth, Sunderland (built in 2017), their dementia-friendly care home in Winnersh near Wokingham (2016) and Abbeyfield Bristol and Keynsham Society's new developments.

All these schemes were designed to incorporate as many as possible of the 'top ten' built environment requirements (detailed in Woodward and Kartupelis, 2018, pp. 149–150). Many of these guidelines are listed below, with responses and comments from the scheme manager about how they are working in practice.

Guideline

To provide residents with variety and choice, at least two communal rooms should be provided in a small home and at least three in a larger home.

Response

'There is always activity in the main lounge. The second lounge tends to get used mostly in the evenings when the men retire to the smaller lounge and the women stay in the main lounge. If the football is on, then it's the other way round. The second lounge has become the "quiet lounge" and a sanctuary. In addition, the local church group use the second lounge as it is away from the main lounge that can get quite noisy.

In the main lounge, there was often bickering about sitting in particular seats or wanting to sit with a particular group of people. The staff change the furniture layout regularly because of this.'

Guideline

A garden room such as an orangery or conservatory should be considered.

Response

'Having direct access to the garden room and outside area is also hugely important for residents, many of whom spend much of their day within the house. Connecting with nature, feeling sunshine and a warm breeze on their face, seeing spring bulbs come up, watching birds and squirrels visiting the feeding tables, noting when the pears and apples are ready for picking – all of this adds to a wonderful feeling of contentment, of being in the right place at this stage of their lives.'

Guideline

A sheltered outdoor space such as a summerhouse should be provided in the garden to encourage residents to maximise their time in the garden.

Response

'Here at Abbeyfield Winnersh we have a lovely big secure garden and two summer houses, both with toilets and one with a kitchenette. Both the summer houses we are planning to open this spring. One we will use as a Vintage Tea Shop, where residents and their families can come and visit and have afternoon tea and cake and look around the summer house, which will be decorated with vintage pictures and memorabilia. The second summer house we are aiming more towards an activities area to include a train set amongst other activities with a slant towards a "man cave" to more support our gentleman here. Both the summer houses will promote the feeling that residents are going out and will enjoy the short walk through the garden to reach them.'

Guideline

Dining rooms should be designed to maximise natural light with attractive views out into the garden and beyond to ensure a pleasant experience, with plenty of light for the visually impaired.

Response

'The need to have natural light and good ventilation in dining areas is absolutely essential. The creation of an airy, spacious environment stimulates appetite and a heightened sense of their surroundings for our residents (many of whom have some degree of visual impairment) and encourages them to linger after meals, thereby promoting increased opportunity for sociability and enhancing well-being.'

Guideline

The lounge should be family-oriented, with access to safe drinks preparation by occupants.

Response

'The main lounge has an area for making tea and coffee. It is used throughout the day by residents, their families and visitors. Residents do like to be able to offer a cup of tea to guests – anyone visiting. It is the main focus of the lounge.'

Guideline

Staff should have a peaceful retreat away from residents to enjoy their breaks.

Response

'There are two staff areas in the property. The one that is used the most is next to the kitchen. It is the kitchen staff room but is used by most staff for a break and to eat their lunch. It is very peaceful and allows staff to get away from residents who can be hard work sometimes.

The other staff room is between two apartments and staff tend not to use it because they fear being overheard.' *(This second comment is worth bearing in mind for future design.)*

Guideline

Whilst efficient, long straight corridors should be avoided wherever possible to ensure that circulation spaces do not feel institutional.

Response

'The corridors at Silksworth do have alcoves which help to break up the view down a corridor but these have been wasted space so far. The staff are currently planning some fundraising to convert these to a reading area/library and a sewing area.'

The future of relational care in residential settings

Before considering the future of the residential model, it should be borne in mind that the great majority of people over 65 live in mainstream housing: 93% according to Age UK (2018). There is a great variation across the spectrum of residential settings, from sheltered housing where people own their homes and can choose what care they wish to buy in, but have communal areas and activities available to them, right through to high-dependency nursing homes. However, the nature of the setting will dictate to what extent a resident can control their daily life. A changing demographic of more active 'young old' and also an increasing number of very frail 'old old' citizens will inevitably influence not only provision and expectations but also the advent of new models of care.

For example, just as care homes have their roots in the institutions designed to cater for those leaving hospital (and also in the Victorian Workhouses), co-housing for older people may appear to be a more recent phenomenon but has its roots in the alms houses movement and charities such as Abbeyfield, which was based on the original idea of its founder Richard Carr Gomm: to help older people take control of their lives and finances by coming together in small groups in a 'family house' and appointing a domestic manager.

Co-housing is a subset of wider 'co-living' arrangements, co-living being the combination of private living spaces with communal facilities. Co-housing adds to this arrangement the aspect of resident-led governance and management. The UK Co-housing Network web site suggests that it offers a ready-made social network that is particularly valuable to certain groups at risk of loneliness, including older people. Schemes such as Older Women's Co-Housing (OWCH) are leading the way with a complex of 25 accessible homes in Barnet (north London) designed around shared gardens, living room and laundry. The emphasis is on residents having control over the development and agreeing their own rules; as reported in *The Guardian* (Robert Booth, 14.7.2019), residents find it 'liberating' in comparison to traditional retirement villages where they would have to accept the prevailing rules of the freeholder.

Co-housing may be one of the ways forward in finding a model that will tempt older people to leave unsuitably large family homes in favour of something they perceive as a positive choice; as the next chapter will outline, there are others such as intergenerational housing and 'villages with care' that enable people with cognitive impairment to participate more fully in community life. Models may vary, but there is no reason why relational care and mutual support, autonomy and purpose in life should not inform their future development.

Learning points from this chapter

- The best type of family home cannot be totally replicated, but its atmosphere, warmth and care can be recreated in new and no less valid ways

- Finding a home that offers good relational care is possible (see below in 'Further Reading' for the factors to consider) and the benefits for an older person and their family and friends can be very significant
- Feeling valued and accepted is very powerful – the knowledge that one is cared 'about' rather than 'for' – and this applies to everyone in a community, not only older people
- The manager of a care home plays a critical role in setting the tone and creating the conditions for everyone to flourish; the recruitment process for this role should be rigorous and if possible involve the residents
- Staff in care homes need similar types of support that older people do: care and recognition as individuals, validation of who they are and what they achieve (through pay, training and advancement), rotas that accommodate time to be with residents and spaces for privacy
- While people are always the most important part of relational care, the physical environment has an important part to play in supporting relationships
- It is important to bring the outside in, in terms of outdoors, outings and local community engagement; and to avoid inadvertently creating a closed community
- Common sense and an openness to new ideas allow health and safety issues to be incorporated into daily living, not become a barrier to it
- Innovation, both technically and in terms of imaginative approaches, can overcome many obstacles to enabling mutual contribution and the feeling that everyone 'belongs' and matters
- A 'whole team' approach enables a wider and more engaged support network but means accepting that time input may be used in ways additional to the primary task of a particular role
- Recruiting for attitude and capacity to develop are more important for staff success and retention than recruiting for qualifications – reduced staff turnover has relational and financial benefits
- Attracting and retaining volunteers (who may be or have been family of residents) offer an excellent resource of time and diversity of interests/capability to extend relationships
- Investing time, thought and innovation into care homes does require commitment to the long haul from owners and charities, but investment brings the rewards of a stable, high-reputation organisation less likely to encounter problems and better fitted to meet them

Some further reading related to this chapter

Care homes: resources for bringing people together

Promoting positive mental wellbeing for older people: A quick guide for registered managers of care homes, Social Care Institute for Excellence, February 2020

NAPA (National Activities Providers Association) is a charity that offers ideas and advice on activities and outings, and practice guides including Developing Community Links, How 'Community Aware' Is Your Care Setting? and Getting Out and About. https://napa-activities.co.uk

The Senses Framework

Poster summary https://www.sheffield.ac.uk/polopoly_fs/1.811379!/file/Senses_Framework_Posters.pdf

Co-Housing

Descriptions and assessments on various models for co-living can be found in *Is Co-living a Housing Solution for Vulnerable Older People?* Quinio and Burgess (2019), Cambridge Centre for Housing and Planning Research.

What to look for in a home

Guidance on matters to consider when visiting a care home and assessing it for yourself or a loved one is given in *Developing a Relational Model of Care* (Woodward and Kartupelis, 2018, pp. 145–148).

4

NEW WAYS OF PROVIDING RELATIONAL CARE

Changing attitudes to relational care

Even small alterations and re-focussing in a care programme or home can renew lives, having significant effects on feelings of mutual support, improved autonomy and contentment and of being valued and loved; but other changes can be more radical and far-reaching.

'Making lives meaningful in old age is new. It therefore requires more imagination and invention than making them merely safe does' (Gawande, 2014, p. 137). Starting from scratch with a new build home allows for one type of innovation, but there are also completely new approaches that do not demand a great deal of alteration to the premises, but rather a major re-assessment and alteration to the whole model of care delivery.

These are approaches that prioritise the key criteria of relational care through instituting new practices, which in turn means reviewing some of the environmental factors so they fully support the change. They can then restore independence, foster new ways of belonging and open up different futures and hopes.

BELONGING SOMEWHERE AND BEING KNOWN

'[Older people] share their life experiences, or they give you knowledge and that empowers them. It's not just about us giving them something' (project manager).

'They're really good' 'They know your history?' 'I think they all do, the whole team' (client).

> 'When I come in and talk about my baby and show pictures, it's nice. It's about how you look at a relationship – so often people think being professional isn't about talking about personal things' (team manager).
>
> 'When a new resident arrives, there will be a bunch of people keen to support them. It's great. It gives that person a sense of "I belong"' (team manager).
>
> 'Why would people open up to you? It needs to be two-way' (carer).
>
> 'They know me, and I have definitely got to know them [the project team] as well. They've become friends' (client).
>
> 'I offered to help and one of the team came with me. We struck up a friendship and I put my trust in her. Made a big difference' (client).

Major changes in outlook and practice enable the empowerment of older people and carers alike.

> I once visited a 106 year old woman who was living with her daughter [who] said I must not hand a book or whatever to her mother for she has to take them herself … I thought this was not very kind until I realised it … was based on the wish not to deprive her mother of the power to do things for herself.
>
> *(Ursula King in Jewell, 2004, p. 138)*

With empowerment comes the confidence and resilience to sustain relationships by encouraging 'adaptive attitudes' (Mowat and Mowat, 2018, p. 174).

'We have at last entered an era in which an increasing number of professionals believe their job is not to confine people's choices, in the name of safety, but to expand them, in the name of living a worthwhile life' (Gawande, 2014, p. 141).

The Montessori approach and older people

The nature of the Montessori approach

Many people are familiar with the Montessori approach in the context of childhood education: schools around the world have been established on the principles of Dr Maria Montessori. These principles espouse independence, autonomy in choices and activities, meaningful engagement and creating an environment where everyone is valued and has a role. Montessori is about empowering people to contribute as fully as they can to their community and can apply equally well to older people.

Anne Kelly, Director of Montessori Consulting based in Australia, has pioneered transferring this approach to aged care, particularly for those living with dementia, and it has now become a global movement. She explains the basis and ethos of the approach:

> In aged care services, we create excess disability when we over-care for people … such as using a wheelchair to take people to the dining room when they could actually walk themselves or feeding people who are able to feed themselves. In Montessori, we focus on a model that enables people to have the time to make true choices, and to have the time to be independent as possible. We think of Montessori staff as being enablers and supporters, enabling people to be the best that they can be and supporting people to be independent.
>
> (Elder Magazine, *undated, accessed February 2020 on web site elder.org*)

Montessori Consulting offers advice and training around the world, and the first UK care home group to pick up the baton was Milford Care, a small privately owned group of six care homes in Nottinghamshire and Derbyshire established in 1985. The Montessori approach is now being actively considered or instituted by others, another early adopter being Hallmark Care Homes, and the information given below reflects meetings with Kelly and with managers, staff and older people in the Milford and Hallmark care homes that I visited.

Montessori appeals to owners and managers of care homes who already see the value of relational care, as it is based on very similar values of validating individuals and creating mutual support based on respect and love. Adopting the ethos and philosophy requires a considerable input of time and change of attitude, and Milford Homes believe it takes about two years to embed the whole process. The most significant cost is training and, possibly, building in more carer/older person interactive time. As one manager said: 'The only real financial implication so far is the costs of the training – a big investment for our group.' The cost of adapting the environment need not be high, as we will see.

The key factor in empowering is the use of techniques to retrain the brain such that an individual can re-start doing simple tasks by improving motor skills rooted in the unconscious memory. The opposite side of this coin is breaking the tasks themselves down into small, manageable parts. One such task was described to me, the 'scooping exercise':

> We put plastic balls in a tub and ask residents to scoop them into an empty tub.… One lady who had a stroke was losing the ability to feed herself and losing weight. We did this work with her and she started to feed herself again and her weight went up. Then she lost a close friend and her weight plummeted – grief – but staff kept going and she gradually gained it again.

Insofar as the environment is concerned, signage is one of the critical factors. It has to be made absolutely clear what each item and room are intended for, by labelling in writing and with graphics, using strong contrast between image and background. For example, if people can easily identify what is in each of their drawers, they can choose clothes themselves; if they were used to washing with a bar of soap previously, but now (for hygiene reasons) have to use a soap dispenser, it must be made clear by labelling that this is for hand washing. But it is not just about clarity of information improving autonomy of performing functions, it is also about encouraging people to act for themselves by choice, so signage also encourages, for example, helping oneself to a drink or piece of fruit, picking up a length of knitting to work on or sitting down at a half-finished jigsaw to 'help us do a bit more of it'. However, too much signage has the potential to become confusing or even distressing, so must be part of an overall, carefully thought through Montessori plan, rather than an 'add-on'.

Both these aspects, regaining skills and having the support of clear directions and invitations, encourage residents to use 'procedural memory' rather than 'declarative memory' – that is, to draw on their long-term memory of 'how to do things', such as walking or tying shoelaces, without referring to conscious awareness, rather than the memory of facts and events explicitly recalled. This creates a setting that 'enhances privacy, dignity and life', as one manager said. 'Montessori gives you the understanding to take a step back and think, *what does that person want to achieve?*'

Not only are good staff training and ongoing support essential but also a different approach to recruitment; for example, in its advertisements, Milford Care describes its homes as places where 'people live and work together' and that they are not looking for 'qualified professionals who are reactive to tasks [but] for Companions who can share emotions, laugh, and make each day fun'.

While the Montessori approach to ageing care was originally developed primarily for those living with dementia and their carers, the underlying principles make sense for any care situation and have the potential to be developed and to further promote relational care. Some groups, such as Hallmark Care Homes, are investigating this and have so far found that piloting the approach indicates it does indeed support relational care. For instance, the way that some of the activities are presented encourages family and friends to participate and strengthen positive relationships.

One specific example is the 'grab and go' station that houses a variety of activities with instructions based on the Montessori principle, which can be quickly picked up by a visitor, completed with their loved one and returned to its place for the next person. The principle also inspires ideas to help residents find their favoured role in contributing to home life, which in turn gives a sense of purpose, belonging and community. For example, the man who delivers the newsletter to all residents, the lady who makes tea for others and clears away at the end, the 'group welcomer' in the 'Songs and Smiles' sessions (described later in this chapter) who welcomes children and their parents into their home.

The Montessori approach to ageing also has good potential to be applied to domiciliary care, as Anne Kelly says:

> Montessori makes a considerable difference for people living at home. If we put in good person-centred care right from early [dementia], then people

are able to stay at home longer ... We can use task breakdown for people to be able to dress themselves or in somebody's bathroom to enable them to go to the toilet themselves. We can put in place fine motor skill activities, to keep somebody with the skills to be able to feed themselves.

(Ibid.)

In this case there would need to be practitioners available to work on the 'fine motor skills' improvement that has happened in the pioneering care homes cited above, and the Maria Montessori Institute in the UK provides this. They report that their two-day initial training workshops apply equally to domiciliary and residential carers, and that about 65% of the uptake is by carers working in family situations, some of whom may be in paid employment. However, they are not aware of any Local Authorities or employers of home carers making bookings.

What the Montessori approach for older people looks like

Walking into a care home that is running on Montessori principles, one immediately feels a sense of purpose and activity with few older people just sitting idly or wandering around: those walking are stopping to speak to others or heading for a specific goal such as a drinks dispenser; those seated are mostly occupied in some way, either individually or as a group. The décor is bright, homely with plenty of small tables, comfortable chairs and windows, books and pictures residents have drawn; there is a 'clean mess' of items around. As I walked around homes when I visited, older people and staff spoke to me and we stopped to talk, but it was also possible to find quiet spaces for the interviews.

The manager of one home met me in the entrance hall, where there was seating and some older people were watching the comings and goings, rather than in his office; he was much in demand for a chat and to deal with queries, and it was clear he was part of the fabric and 'family' of the home. Indeed, it was very much a family space, with a few younger people visiting relatives. This was not a place of despair, nor of people just biding their time.

Anne Kelly says:

Not only organisations but families are starting to realise that there's more to quality of life than the curtains matching the furnishings and everything being neat and tidy.... often the people we're building for are not the people who need to live in them, but the families who make decisions about where people go ... quality of life is more than a nice environment. It's about having a reason to get out of bed, and that's about everybody feeling valued and that their life matters.

(Ibid.)

Homes introducing the Montessori approach can often overcome the apparent constraints on the factors that favour it. For example, one wanted to encourage residents to cook and bake but could not give them access to the main kitchen without supervision, nor provide individual ovens, so they organised small group sessions with a member of staff and then that group could share the cakes they made over a cup of tea.

Impacts

Hallmark Homes undertook a three-month pilot in four of their homes, starting with two full training days for the staff involved. They tracked impacts before and after using a dementia care mapping exercise, the Cohen- Mansfield Agitation Inventory (short form), to capture changes in behaviour, and a reading screening assessment to identify additional measures that may be required by individuals to make the environment more enabling, positive and supportive. After the pilot they noted that the biggest impacts appeared to have been achieved through the development of reading groups, changes to the environment (with team members able to evidence this with photographs) and ensuring meaningful occupation. Short case studies were written up to illustrate the positive impacts of Montessori methods.

Additionally, sections of the Inventory showed the greatest changes were:

• 22% reduction in cursing or verbal aggression
• 32% decrease in constant calling out
• 31% reduction in general signs of restlessness
• 23% reduction in pacing/walking

Montessori Consulting have noted from their own observations that adopting the approach leads to fewer falls, less use of psychotropic drugs and dietary supplements, as well as better sleep, less anxiety and aggression and greater staff and carer satisfaction.

There are plans to evaluate overall the introduction of the Montessori approach in the UK, and at present, funding is being sought to commission a university to undertake this.

What does the Montessori approach feel like in practice?

Adopting this model greatly helps a domiciliary team or care home to fulfil the conditions for good relational care. I interviewed residents, staff and managers in two care homes practising the approach, where the environmental and attitudinal changes had been embedded and ongoing training was in progress. The quotes below help with understanding what the approach feels like for the people involved.

ADOPTING MONTESSORI PRINCIPLES AND VALUES

'This [Montessori] is something we're working on introducing at the moment. I wasn't familiar with it and a lot of people see it from the school perspective, but in fact some bits we were doing without realising it. It makes sense in so many ways' (activities co-ordinator).

'Staff are trained to walk around with residents; they'll say, "What does this say? Take a piece of fruit, would you like to?" So they take one and it improves their nutrition' (regional manager).

'There's a difference between clean and untidy, organised mess as opposed to dirty mess. I like stuff everywhere because people can pick it up and engage' (home manager).

Building relationships of trust and being known

'They [residents] give you their trust and will open up to you' (carer).

'The one thing someone wants is reassurance, the touch of the face, holding the hand' (manager).

'A few of us sit together; I never eat in my room. The meals are so good!' (resident).

'The staff are having one-to-one training and learning all the time about improving their practice with Montessori, and they're learning more about the residents because they're communicating much better' (regional manager).

Enabling greater autonomy and life purpose

'One lady used to wander around looking quite tearful. One of her jobs had been in a school dining room, so we asked her to help clear the tables' (team manager).

'People like to contribute. One lady likes to peel the potatoes' (manager).

'We have a small book club now; our aim is to get residents and families to run book clubs themselves' (regional manager).

'We encourage residents to take a little bit of risk by supporting them. You are about protecting and caring but not restricting' (regional manager).

'Now you're doing more things [activities]. Does that help you in looking after yourself, like getting dressed, or was that okay anyway?'

'It's definitely helped' (interviewer/resident).

'People are getting more involved; a few like to collect the coffee cups up, [name] puts them on her tray on her walker and pushes them along. You like to help out?'

'Yes, I think so' (carer/resident).

'One lady's daughter said, "My mum always wore a housecoat and had dusters in her pockets" so we gave her those and now she spends lots of time dusting. She's very occupied and has purpose' (manager).

Addressing isolation

'I like music and singing'
'Do carers join in sometimes?'
'Oh yes, it's a friendly place' (resident/interviewer).
'The other people here are friendly, and I'm so pleased about that. We're all quite friendly' (resident).
'We adapt activities so that people find it easier to join in' (activities co-ordinator).

Working with the wider community

'We ask local groups in; we want the community to know we are here' (manager).

Benefits to staff

'Montessori principles have changed our approach to recruitment. We're saying we want people to come and be part of the residents' lives, come into their home' (manager).

'I have to learn to work with their abilities and strengths; the Montessori training, it helps them to contribute more to life here, getting them to understand that they can still do things' (activities co-ordinator).

'If the team are happy, it's much easier for them to make the residents and families happier' (activities co-ordinator).

Learning points

The main learning points for embedding Montessori principles in a home or community team practice can be summarised as follows.

- Owners of schemes or homes have to acknowledge that this will entail a significant investment in training over at least two years as well as ongoing staff support
- There also has to be a change of thinking on the part of everyone involved, focussing not on what people cannot or should not do but on what they can do
- Re-imagining the physical space of the place where older people are living (their own or a care home) is important; to continually be asking, 'Is it easy and inviting to access the items and information they need for self-care?

- Activities must be directed towards helping people achieve their purpose; and identifying that purpose by getting to know them well

Intergenerational practice, older people and relational care

The value of young people being involved in the lives of older ones was cited in Chapter 1 as a key criterion of relational care. In theory, this should be something that happens naturally in families and communities; in practice, it may well not. In recent years there have been a number of initiatives intended to improve intergenerational contact and, most importantly, to nurture relationships that will benefit all involved. The social enterprise 'United for All Ages', whose concern that Britain is one of the most age-segregated countries in the world has led it to campaign for recognition of the problem and its solutions, implements, supports and promotes a range of projects developing intergenerational care, housing, health, learning and centres across the country. Their web site is an excellent source of ideas and information.

There are now a considerable number of initiatives in the UK with nursery and school age children and with young adults, and as we will see, they have the potential to nurture and promote good relational care by enabling many of the key criteria. For the purposes of this chapter, I will be looking in detail at two examples of nurseries and pre-school groups co-located with care homes: Nightingale House and Wren Hall, the care home described in the previous chapter. The possibilities for community-based interaction with young children will also be addressed. There then follows a consideration of an intergenerational co-housing project in Cambridge and similar projects from which wider learning can be taken.

The examples chosen are clearly not comprehensive, and many more exist, either established or getting under way, with some more successful than others; but they do offer tried-and-tested examples of good practice, give a feeling for what it is like to be involved in them and provide key learning points for those considering similar ideas.

Intergenerational projects involving children

The concept of bringing young children and older people together

Projects may be set up by care homes on their own premises or by bringing children into the home in an organised way (as opposed to the casual visits we looked at in the previous chapter); or projects may be attached to community-based teams such as Neighbourhood Cares, which was cited in Chapter 2.

In the former category, one of the best known is the Apples and Honey nursery attached to Nightingale House, a faith-based care home in South West London, with around 185 residents in different households, established by the Jewish charity Nightingale Hammerson over 175 years ago. The nursery was opened in 2017 as a social enterprise, and interaction between children and older people takes place through a weekly programme of events. These include residents visiting the nursery to participate as much or little as they wish in activities such as singing, playtime and storytelling; and children visiting areas of the home daily, not only to meet residents and get to know individuals but also to take part in and learn about the basic practices of Judaism. Early learning skills are developed together through buddied reading, joint exercise classes and numberwork, and history is brought alive through the lived memories of the residents.

Wren Hall in Nottinghamshire set up the Little Wrens nursery and pre-school in 2018, and it is designed to be a 'home from home' and to be closely integrated with the care lounges. So the nursery has its own space, including a forest school, and its own qualified staff, but the children also spend regular, daily time with the residents in their own accommodation where they can undertake joint activities such as singing, dancing and baking and in a large interactive garden shared by both sites. Whilst these two examples are by no means the only establishments in the UK that have adopted this model, they have been pioneers and are assisting the learning of newcomers to the concept.

Some care homes are using external advisers to help them build links with nearby nurseries or schools; for example, The Together Project was set up in 2017 to set up parent and toddler groups specially to visit care homes and undertake musical and other intergenerational activities that build regular interaction, with benefits for three generations: children, parents/staff and older people. Their first programme, 'Songs and Smiles', has been developed by talking with and listening carefully to older people taking part in the pilot and now currently runs in 13 care homes a week, primarily in North East London. It is not based in schools or nurseries; children come into the care home with a parent or guardian, with the intended advantage of creating good links with the local community.

The programme is run by and for the community, with a vital network of volunteers who range from a specialist music therapist, who has co-designed the format, to people who have struggled to connect with their communities in the past through homelessness or long-term health problems and are now looking for a way to become part of something meaningful. The financial model is based on payment by homes that are able to do so and grant funding being sought for those who do not have the resources to do so.

There is also the possibility of community-based projects for adults linking with local schools. Inspired by the Channel 4 series 'Old People's Home for 4-year-olds' screened in 2017, and their knowledge of the risk of isolation for older and vulnerable people, the Soham Neighbourhood Cares team – described in detail in Chapter 2 – decided to test the viability in their home town for a similar link as part of their wider community cohesion offering. In order to do so, a partnership project group was formed to include a Primary School, a Retirement Living Scheme, Soham Children's Centre, the Care Network charity and the Neighbourhood Cares Team.

Ten older people considered at risk of loneliness and ten reception-age children without nearby older relatives were selected and brought together in four one-hour pilot sessions of simple activities, song and getting to know one another and build relationships. The sessions were conducted in a communal room in the retirement living scheme and overseen by a Higher-Level Teaching Assistant; safeguarding measures were put in place in advance.

What intergenerational projects with young children look like

While the embedded nurseries in care homes such as Nightingale House and Wren Hall may be established for various reasons, including concerns about isolation, knowledge of similar schemes, responses to local and internal staff needs for good nursery care, good examples have much in common in terms of their effect on the atmosphere of the home and on the people involved. Having visited both these schemes several times, and other homes with intergenerational projects, and talked to residents, managers, staff and parents, these interviews, together with evaluation reports, form a consistent picture of all generations benefiting from across-age interaction.

When a care home is part of intergenerational practice, what the visitor is most likely to notice initially is that people are having fun and few are sitting around looking depressed. There is a liveliness in the atmosphere, which cannot just be ascribed to the actual presence of children but also their past and future presence. For example, walls are decorated with youngsters' pictures, there is evidence of crafts lying around and there are colourful posters about future activities.

The nursery areas are also light and bright, with a feeling of being part of the outside, filled with noise, interaction and most likely music or singing. Small children may be sitting on the laps of older people or have their heads together with them, absorbed in painting or playing with dolls, model cars or picture books. Helpers and parents may be engaged in conversation with each other or with the residents. It is an energising atmosphere and in Little Wrens, for example – in common with the care home to which it is attached – all those involved see themselves as part of a 'family' group.

'The entire feel of the care home is lighter, filled with a new range of sounds (mainly laughter from nursery children), and there is a deep sense of community between all the age groups, staff, family members, volunteers and residents. The intergenerational programme has become a glue that brings the different parts of the care home together' (*The Intergenerational Programme at Nightingale House: A Study into the Impact on the Well-being of Elderly Residents*, Somers, A, executive summary, March 2019, p. 9).

Impacts

It can be seen from the descriptions above that intergenerational projects help to meet at least some of the key criteria for relational care and that some meet nearly all of them. Not surprisingly, therefore, these intergenerational initiatives involving children are very likely to deliver the benefits of relational care to older people and staff, as well as advantages to the children and parents. Interestingly Nightingale House has adopted as one of its Key Performance Indicators, the level of support for relationship-centred care.

The evaluation study of Nightingale House and Apples and Honey includes a list of 'observable benefits' (ibid., p. 7) to older people that can be summarised as follows:

- Opportunity to be part of something wider and to look outward rather than inward; fresh topics of conversation with staff and families
- Friendly and affirmative interactions, and sustained relationships, addressing social isolation and depression
- Passive and active cognitive stimulation through participation in, and observation of play
- Reminiscence and stimulation of memories (particularly valuable to those with dementia)
- Improved ability to contribute to the 'community' by helping and encouraging children, sharing learning and experience with them
- Increase in physical movement improving co-ordination, balance and strength (all generally associated with, for example, reduction in falls)

The Wren Hall project had not yet undergone a formal evaluation, but interviews with staff and parents indicated that in their experience, it yielded just the same type of impacts and benefits to older people as those noted above. Louise Goulden, the founder of Together CIC, has recorded very similar impacts in her funding applications and notes. These include the point that, although its programmes are not specifically directed at those with dementia, she has observed that they are a group which particularly benefits; just as Somers did in her report.

Insofar as the Soham community-based project is concerned, there has been an internal evaluation. All the older people who took part had a discussion with one of the project leaders and completed a pre- and post-pilot assessment about their quality of life, with the intention that it would be possible to evidence changes in their emotional and physical health. The children did not participate in a formal evaluation but through conversations in class, before, during and after the programme together with feedback from parents and teachers, the impact of their involvement on their confidence and behaviour was assessed. There were some small differences in the scores for several of the residents, usually in an upward trajectory, but the group leaders believed that factors other than participation influenced the scores, especially ill health. They judged that the questionnaire was of limited value and that evidence of impact was probably more effectively derived primarily from qualitative conversations and from observation.

The impacts discussed above are specifically concerned with the older people involved, although in the case of Nightingale House, there are plans to evaluate the benefits to children using accepted methodology. From my studies at both

Nightingale and Wren Hall, as well as talking to other homes and external providers together with considering the report on the Neighbourhood Cares community project, I would add that there appear to be appreciable benefits to all participants, namely:

Children

- Improved confidence, social skills, empathy and behaviour
- Improved verbal skills
- More willingness to initiate conversations with adults
- Enriching relationships with a different generation (particularly valuable to those otherwise without regular contact with elders)
- Opportunity to discover new modes of play and interaction
- In the case of the community-based project, parents at the school asked for their children to take part in future projects

Staff (and relatives of older people)

- More positive interactions with older people, because they receive more stimulation and enjoy new interests, feel less isolated and have improved wellbeing
- Additional areas of 'common ground' with older people and other staff (particularly if they are also parents of the children)
- Extending their skill sets by working as a team with professionals from different age expertise
- Enjoyment of seeing and being with the children; happier and livelier atmosphere

Parents

- Children are finding interactions and relationships in school and family easier to negotiate
- They may form relationships with older people whom they get to know as part of their children's lives

In the context of relational care, two points from the Nightingale evaluation cited above underline the value of consistent, long term: 'Benefits build up over time. Residents who regularly socialise with nursery children report significant improvements in mental health and well-being' (2019, p. 9) and 'Regular contact between the same children and residents had the greatest impact' (ibid., p. 10).

What do intergenerational projects with young children feel like?

Listening to the voices of participants brings the concept to life and demonstrates how it can deliver relational care; the following are from interviews undertaken for this book and from an internal evaluation of the Soham community project.

BUILDING RELATIONSHIPS OF TRUST AND BEING KNOWN

'More children need an opportunity to form a positive, healthy relationship with older people' (parent).

'[My child] built a relationship with one resident through activities, who was known for not wanting to get engaged, and staff were taken aback that she responded so positively when they were paired up' (parent).

'Around older people children start off by being nervous, but they very quickly create relationships' (manager).

He [my child] has a special bond with Michael; they'll sit and talk together and play with diggers. This relationship happened quite naturally' (parent).

'Whenever she saw [my child] she would smile, I had to lift her up as this lady sits in a special wheelchair and normally communicates through limited facial expressions' (parent).

'The older ones [children] will share what they've been doing' (resident).

'The older people and children taught each other new songs' (community project leader).

'With the nursery children you get to know the parents as well; they're lovely' (resident).

'One of the residents talks to her about her day, they always remember her and ask about her' (parent/carer).

'If she's in a mood, she will show it, whatever she's feeling, good or bad, she's not reserved, she feels comfortable enough with them [the residents] to express that' (parent).

'They [child and older person] have very affectionate interchanges' (parent).

Older people said that they had something to chat to their families about' (community project leader).

'We've tried it in the past, getting different generations in, but you must have the continuity, or it's hard to build relationships' (activities manager).

Enabling greater autonomy, contribution and life purpose

'Older people said they felt it gave them a reason to get up in the morning' (community project leader).

'She [my child] reads with the residents; it's learning from someone more experienced who can offer a different way of teaching. If the resident used to be a headmistress, a teacher, then they can provide the skills I wouldn't have' (parent).

'It brings back a dimension into your life, how things started, how young children act and react' (resident)

'One morning I went over to the nursery to read a story. Instead of getting one of their books out, I told a personal anecdote about my niece. I told them the whole story, they loved it' (resident)

'It definitely uplifts the resident; we've seen a complete change in body language, in facial expression' (parent/carer).

'Memories flooded back of when I used to work in a school' (older person).

'Adults lost their concerns about their ability to get involved in some of the physical activities and took part' (community project leader).

'These small people bring a new lease of life' (carer).

'One striking benefit for the elderly care home residents was relief from being the object of care... and feeling disempowered and passive. The introduction of children into the setting reverses roles' (Somers in Nightingale evaluation report p. 8).

Addressing isolation and depression

'Interactions are so important for this resident as she suffers from depression and needs an outlet; even if it's a toddler running around, she's so comfortable with her being around' (carer).

'Their smiley faces made me smile' (older person).

'They [the children] bring joy to lots of people. There are people who don't wish to join in' (resident).

'It made me feel younger' (older person).

'It's made a difference to our lives; it's lovely.' 'Makes you realise you were once like that' (two residents in conversation).

'We enjoy them. Gradually they get to know you, look your way and give you a smile and you notice it' (resident).

Benefits to children

'It's good for her to have an appreciation of the elderly and have relationships with different people, have friendships. It's very enriching for her' (parent).

'It helps her build confidence and communication skills, to sit and talk to people and listen to how their day is going' (parent/carer).

'It has improved my child's relationships with other children, he has more confidence, he has definitely got this from being with the older people, I don't worry about him so much' (parent).

'He [my child] has much greater confidence; he's not a natural leader but now needs much less reassurance' (parent).

'He [my child] now interacts better with his peers and is developing as an individual' (parent).

'When I left her [her daughter] there, I thought there would be tears, but it wasn't like that. On Monday she waved me goodbye, and she's loved it ever since' (parent).

Benefits to staff

'Children also have an effect on the staff; they feel very positive about watching the interactions, brings them joy' (parent).

Working with the wider community

'The project created links and more ideas for partnership work between agencies inspired by working together' (community project leader).

'We have an intergenerational music group that comes in very frequently and we have group singing sessions. We can form those unique bonds [with the local community] (manager).

'Some older people were considering being helpers in school, listening to children read' (community project leader).

'We did have a link with a local school, but we can see that we need to build more of a bond with residents, more interactive' (manager).

'We've started a pen pal scheme with a local school to try to form relationships. Hopefully they will start to form, the same resident with the same child. It's a slow burner' (activities manager).

Learning points

The following key points are drawn from visits, interviews and evaluation reports.

- Longevity of the project and the relationships formed is critical to reaping the full benefits: projects should be set up with this in mind, rather than as an additional short-term 'experience' for any of the parties
- In the same way, there should be consistency and routine in the programme of interactions, a commitment to attend unless prevented by ill health
- Intergenerational encounters can be successful in the nursery school or residential home setting
- There needs to be a good balance in numbers for group sessions: sufficient children that all older people can interact, but not so many that they become overwhelming
- Each session must be long enough to allow participants to get settled in
- Activities need to be engaging and have active elements to encourage participation

- Early years teachers, care staff and therapists should all be involved as a team in planning and delivering sessions, and learning from one another
- Parents should be involved and consulted
- People with dementia should be at least as much involved as other older people
- Older people should be assessed individually for their support needs and the likely benefits, and where possible, they should be fully involved in offering ideas and feedback

Intergenerational projects involving young and older adults

While there is a deficit in Britain in terms of interaction between children and older people, there is arguably an even greater deficit where young adults and their grandparents' generation are concerned. The projects described in the section above clearly create environments where relational care could flourish and yield benefits to all concerned, but is it also possible to design initiatives involving young adults that will offer similar benefits?

There is a relatively small number of these projects currently established in the UK, and others at pilot stage or under evaluation. The Intergenerational Housing Network (IHN), a group of interested parties, notes that 'there are relatively few schemes that can genuinely be described as 'intergenerational housing': where different generations live alongside each, can mix and share activities and experiences, with a common purpose. This is despite recognition of the potential benefits of such schemes – from addressing health and social needs to helping tackle the housing crisis and building stronger communities.... in every part of the UK there are opportunities to develop schemes relatively swiftly, using under-occupied sheltered housing as the basis for older people living alongside younger people ... and providing mutual support (see Cambridge, Haringey for examples)' (Submission to APPG on Social Integration, September 2019).

In past centuries, it was not at all unusual for several generations of a family to live together; in fact, as we have seen, it may have been the best or only chance for older relatives to receive care before the advent of the welfare state (although need not imply that care is needed or being provided). The number of multigenerational homes, after being well-nigh written off as an unattractive prospect, is starting to rise in the UK.

> The Office for National Statistics estimates suggest that the number of households with three generations living together had risen from 325,000 in 2001 to 419,000 in 2013.... The total number of all multigenerational households in Britain is thought to be about 1.8 million.
>
> *(report in The Observer, James Tapper, 10 March 2019)*

Returning to the possibility of creating intergenerational living, while there are more models overseas (in the Netherlands or South Africa for example), its growth and potential to support the key criteria for relational care should be recognised. IHN notes barriers to progress as including silo working, lack of strategic approaches, of funding and of innovation and advocates for more joined-up working, commitment and awareness of good models already in existence.

There are several examples of co-housing and home-sharing that involve older people (the Cambridge Centre for Housing and Planning Research (CCHPR) report *Is Co-living a Housing Solution for Vulnerable Older People? Final Report* (Quinio and Burgess, 2019) gives an excellent commentary on each type and its pros and cons). However, CCHPR identified only one Housing Association scheme in the UK that was offering a co-living residential development where younger people share accommodation with older people on which they could undertake an evaluation study.

This was LinkAges, a collaboration between CHS group, a charitable Housing Association in Cambridgeshire and Cambridge Hub, a student-led organisation that aims to create positive social change. The LinkAges initiative, which has now ended after two successful years, was based in one of CHS Group's sheltered housing schemes in Cambridge; three postgraduate students were trained in intergenerational working, project planning, dementia and safeguarding and were placed in flats within the scheme at below-market rent in return for providing 15 hours a week to offer companionship with the aim of improving the health and wellbeing of the existing older residents. The evaluation study, based primarily on in-depth interviews, concluded:

> Intergenerational .... Housing Associations schemes may have the potential to help relatively independent older people who require a moderate amount of additional support in their daily life.... [but they] should not be considered as a replacement for care homes and specialised housing for later life.
>
> *(Ibid., p. 74)*

The benefits for older people were seen as fairly marginal, mainly because the age threshold for the accommodation was 55, so many of them were still going out to work and had limited time for engagement. 'It's always been the same. People go to work; others don't really bother and don't want to join in' (older resident). Also, the presence of the students (and the longevity of the scheme) was relatively short term, limiting relationships and creating some anxiety. 'You don't like to see them going. You get to know them, you get closer, and then it's goodbye, and hello again' (older resident). Some said they enjoyed having the young people around and appreciated help with getting up the stairs or carrying heavy bags, and occasionally sharing coffee or cooking.

The benefits to the students appeared to be greater, with some very enthusiastic about the experience, saying that they were cheered up by having older people around, and it seemed to put their own problems into perspective: 'I find it really easy and enjoyable and it doesn't seem like a job at all!' (student).

Insofar as relational care is concerned, this single study suggests that bringing younger and older adults together does have benefits for both, but to fulfil the majority of the key criteria for relational care, schemes would have to be carefully designed and organised, with suitable communal space, and there would need to be a high level of desire for and commitment to engagement on both sides.

The question of ageism and its deleterious results were addressed in Chapter 1 and will be considered further in terms of its effects on policy. It may be that one of the benefits of young and older adults spending more time together will undermine the false foundations of ageism. For example, in the United States, 'The AARP Disrupt Age campaign paired millennials with older people to unsettle younger people's assumptions about the physical abilities of older people' (Barnes et al. p. 54) and some similar disruption may not go amiss in the UK.

Older people and the company of animals

It would be impossible to review the benefits of older and younger generations being together but neglect the impact of animal interaction. Arguably, this is not a new intervention of the type outlined in the previous sections and could feature anywhere in this book. Perhaps as an animal-lover I am tempted to say that animals should feature everywhere but am aware not everyone would take this viewpoint.

However, for many older people, relationships with animals play an important role in giving meaning to life, encouraging activity, acting as a point of commonality with other people and bringing profound contentment. For them, the presence of an animal is undoubtedly an environmental factor enabling relational care.

It is detrimental to deprive the people who love them of animal company; conversely, enabling their presence can give older people a new lease of life in the way that introducing children into their lives can do. The Society for Companion Animal Studies (SCAS), which provides information and advocacy, says that pets provide:

- Constancy, a sense of purpose and structure to the day
- A sense of empowerment and an opportunity to contribute
- Companionship and friendship – for some older people, pets may be their only friend
- Affection and unconditional love – which helps to bolster self-esteem and self-worth
- Social support – pets can act as social catalysts enabling better person-to-person interactions
- Support during a bereavement – a comforting presence at a time of loneliness

It is interesting to note how closely these benefits match the key criteria for relational care. The resulting impacts are:

- Increase attentiveness to own self-care needs
- Increase nutritional intake in presence of a fish tank
- Increase perception of wellbeing

- Reduce GP consultation for minor ailments
- Reduce blood pressure (presence or stroking)
- Reduce verbal aggression and anxiety in people with Alzheimer's disease
    (source: SCAS web site accessed March 2020 http://www.scas.org.uk/
    human-animal-bond/pets-and-older-people/)

Where older people are living in their own home, they can be assisted to keep and look after a beloved pet by friends, neighbours and charities. For example, Borrow My Doggy, a 'walkies exchange' web site, has teamed up with community schemes such as Didsbury Good Neighbours, which aim to support senior members of the community through a volunteer befriending service and a programme of weekly activities, to help them introduce a canine element into their programme.

If a move to a residential home is needed, the story may be very different. SCAS commissioned a Pets and Older People in Residential Care survey, published in 2008, which found that there had been few improvements in attitude on the part of care homes over the preceding 15 years and that further action was needed. They launched a Pets for Life campaign, urging housing providers to recognise that being parted from a pet can have a devastating impact on health and wellbeing. It has since brought about some change, in particular Conservative MP Nigel Waterson's Care Homes and Sheltered Accommodation (domestic pets) Bill passed in March 2010.

Care homes that exemplify good relational practice, such as those featuring in the previous chapters, do recognise this issue and aim to meet it insofar as possible. Negative arguments about hygiene are difficult to sustain, given that animals are so often part of a family home. Some allow individual residents' pets, but this can create difficulties if the accommodation is unsuitable or other residents may be affected. Therefore they more often have a 'house pet' (usually a cat or dog) who lives in the home and shares its life with everyone there, or volunteers may visit regularly with suitable animals. This does not offer the close individual bond an owner builds with their pet but does bring several of the advantages listed above. Additionally, staff may bring in their own pets to be enjoyed by everyone: 'Dogs brought in by staff or family visitors provide great enjoyment and nearly all residents whom I interviewed put contact with companion animals near the top of their wish list' (Woodward and Kartupelis, 2018, p. 55).

ANIMALS WELCOME

'There's a man here who loves cats; he goes to visit Tommy [the resident cat] every day to stroke him, so I'll go and sit with him and we talk about our pets' (carer).

'The only time I got told off by a resident was when I forgot to take in my dog!' (regional manager).

'People bring in pets as well as children – dogs, even reptiles' (carer).

Area-wide models encouraging relational care

Relational care is a concept that is easier to institute in a relatively small community, given that it is built on networks of mutual knowledge, trust and support. Yet it can be translated into big cities with imagination, civic and personal commitment.

Age Friendly Cities (AFC) originated as a result of a World Health Organisation (WHO) programme and are designed 'to offer more potential for collective action to reconfigure public spaces, transport systems, and buildings in ways that will support older people's social and civic participation' (Barnes et al., 2018, p. 18). Subsequently, the participative research and 'voices' on which their book is based formed an important source of information and ideas for the Brighton and Hove AFC initiative, suggesting it be based not only on the WHO criteria but also on emphasising older people's 'identities as relational beings', whose wellbeing depends on retaining 'a sense that they are valued by others, and can remain connected to things that matter to them' (ibid., p. 169).

Similarly in Leeds the AFC programme is based on the concept of the older person as an active and integral part of the community rather than primarily a care recipient. Leeds is one of UK's largest cities with an estimated and growing population of about 800,000, which has been a member of the WHO Age Friendly Cities Network since 2013. The project 'Making Leeds the Best City to Grow Old In' is enabling a form of relational care to be embedded there. Without going into the detail of all the work and different projects, such as addressing housing and public transport needs and creating accessible outdoor spaces, which have contributed to the Leeds initiative, it is interesting to look at the underlying drivers recognised by the Age Friendly Leeds Partnership as they started their planning. The partnership included Local Authorities, charities, universities and the Centre for Ageing Better.

The drivers arose from citizen-based policy, where the focus is not on the individual as a patient or care recipient, nor on care directed towards the person as an isolated entity, but on the individual as part of a connected society. This shifts the emphasis of programmes development towards building inclusive neighbourhoods, changing negative social attitudes towards age and promoting participation. In fact, the factors that nurture relational care can be extrapolated from the local community or care home and re-interpreted in the city.

The aims of Age Friendly Leeds are to create a city where older people are valued, feel respected and appreciated and are seen as the assets they are. The story of how this is being achieved is a tale of many smaller, localised community development projects as well as city-wide ones, with practical aims and outcomes, strongly supported by volunteers. The initiative and work continue and are accessible on the City Council's web site (see below in the resources section).

The critical role of architecture in creating environments that support relationships was raised in the previous chapter in the context of individual buildings and applies equally to wider urban design; this is an issue on which the RIBA has been working over a period of time. It has brought together its findings and provides a knowledge base on 'age inclusive' design on its web site (see below in the resources section).

Broadening innovation to support relational care

Innovation has much to offer relational care. This chapter has considered new ways of meeting the key criteria to facilitate relationships, and one of the issues to emerge is the potential for technology to create greater opportunities for freedom of movement, autonomy and interpersonal connection. This has already been raised by the review of its use by Dutch organisation tanteLouise, described in Chapter 2. Technical developments can make time-consuming tasks such as recording more efficient and less obtrusive, releasing face-to-face time. But does technical innovation also have the potential to inhibit the formation of bonds by diverting carer focus away from people to screens and data or even an attempt to substitute for human relationships without offering the scope for mutuality? The market for technology in age care is diverse and fast-moving, and the next chapter addresses its role in the context of relational care.

There may be constraints and issues about how much innovation can offer to supporting the age-old need for human connection and love, but as this chapter proposes, there are new possibilities and ideas coming forward, and there will undoubtedly be more fresh approaches to fostering environments in which human bonds and people can thrive; it is certain that imagination need not be a limiting factor.

Some further reading related to this chapter

Intergenerational models

United for All Ages is the UK body for information, news, advice and advocacy: https://www.unitedforallages.com

Housing LIN has information on all types of intergenerational housing: https://www.housinglin.org.uk/Topics/browse/Housing/HousingforOlderPeople/intergenerational-housing/

Montessori model

Montessori Consulting (Australia) for information on applying the Montessori principle to ageing care: https://montessoriconsulting.com.au

Maria Montessori Institute (UK) for training courses in applying the principles to dementia and ageing https://www.mariamontessori.org

Companion animals

Society for Companion Animal Studies is a charity that provides scientific evidence of the benefits of animal-human interactions and promotes the benefits of pet ownership www.scas.org.uk/human-animal-bond/pets-and-older-people/

Cinnamon Trust is a charity that provides practical assistance and advice to older people about retaining and caring for their pets, especially when circumstances become difficult https://cinnamon.org.uk

Borrow My Doggy is a web site that matches owners and dog lovers to arrange walking and care on a voluntary basis, also offers a community of users and advice https://www.borrowmydoggy.com

Age friendly cities: Leeds

Web sites https://www.leeds.gov uk/age-friendly-leeds/what-we-are-doing
   https://timetoshineleeds.org/
   Report *Making Leeds the Best City to Grow Old In*, 2018, Leeds City Council
   The concept and history: World Health Organisation (2007) *Global Age-Friendly Cities: A Guide*, Geneva: WHO Press

Age inclusive design

The RIBA offers a knowledge database on these issues at https://www.zotero.org/groups/234052/riba_research/collections/ITFIKCH2 and a handbook at https://www.architecture.com/knowledge-and-resources/resources-landing-page/age-friendly-handbook

5

TECHNOLOGY

Friend or foe?

Lorraine Morley

Introduction

This chapter looks at the role of technology in ageing and later life living. It first explores the types of technology that are emerging and then gives a brief market survey of developments, applications and why some may be more popular than others. Having provided this context, it then addresses the role of new technologies in relational care and considers current developments and where they might lead in the future.

Many solutions to help support caring and carers have been developed over the last few years with digital products seeing the most prolific increase. There are 350,000 digital health apps alone, many of which are increasingly used to help support and promote healthy ageing. A key question is how technology and innovation that we have now could help us as we advance through the years and in particular how it could help maintain relational bonds, dignity and mutual respect, as well as supporting continued independence at the level appropriate and desired by an individual. This chapter also addresses aspects that need to be carefully considered, such as the right to privacy and self-determination, and also how accessible technologies are, both in terms of complexity and cost.

Much of the information and knowledge in this chapter has emerged from research undertaken as part of an EU-funded project called SEAS2Grow (Silver Economy Accelerating Strategies 2 Grow). The innovation support programme that sits at the heart of the project extends across four countries – UK, France, Belgium and the Netherlands – in which nine partners scout for, identify and support businesses with innovative goods and services for later life living. All the partners in the project have the wellbeing of the older population at their heart. More information about his project can be found at www.agetechaccelerator.com.

Products that have been identified so far and that support ageing can largely be organised into three groups:

- **Informal care** – this includes apps and digital platforms to help families keep in touch remotely and to share care responsibilities as needs evolve. Products are aimed at both the caregiver and the care receiver. Many products in this category appear to have difficulty finding viable business models, scaling up and gaining traction in the market. This could be because the majority of people are used to being offered free downloads, and even if they might consider paying, they often want to try it out first. The Apple store at November 2019 had more than 2 million apps available for download, and according to information from TechCrunch, the technology and start-up reporting website, 90 percent of apps on the market are free. However, that might be changing, and whilst games continue to account for a majority of consumer spending that does happen, trends show that subscription income for non-gaming apps is steadily increasing.
- **Formal care** – this includes products for both domiciliary care providers and care home or nursing home businesses. The focus here is on care management, increasing productivity and efficiency and better reporting. Often the products can track the activities of staff and serve as a window into the quality of care and the wellbeing of the care recipient.
- **Health** – this includes apps, platforms and physical products which track or monitor everyday health conditions. This might be as basic as counting the number of steps taken each day, monitoring weight or quality of sleep or increasingly sophisticated products that verge on the clinical by measuring blood pressure, pulse and breathing and, in combination with a smart phone, can turn into a device to check changes in conditions of eyesight, hearing and balance. There has been a significant increase in the number of platforms offering online consultations with medical professionals.

However, despite the proliferation of choice, the consumer and business-to-business markets remain difficult for many businesses to crack, although technology giants such as Google, Amazon and Facebook are beginning to see the potential of the age tech industry. They are increasingly aware of the opportunity to tap into the world's fastest growing and (at least in the developed world) most wealthy demographic, so we are likely to see a further acceleration, particularly in products and business models based on digital platforms using voice-control and artificial intelligence.

But barriers to adoption and the problems of scaling continue to constrain this emerging market, and those products which might help relational care flourish are not necessarily easy to find or to assess in terms of their validity and efficacy. Part of this problem is that many appear to have been designed and developed in isolation of the environments in which they are supposed to perform. Often, they have been motivated by personal experiences of the developer, of a parent or grandparent suffering from age-related issues such as declining physical or cognitive functionality. It is typical of many investment pitches that they start with a personal story along these lines. While these concerns are very valid, it can mean that the product is developed in isolation from the wider market and without focus on a more generalised need. Often these types of products are app-based and lack a wider value proposition which fails to find a viable business model or market.

Some product areas suffer from oversupply such as apps to help keep older people connected to family, social circles and community; this leads to high level of competitor products but few buyers. On the other hand, those which deal with more practical and less palatable aspects of ageing, such as incontinence, suffer from a lack of product solutions or innovations yet have a ready market.

The speed of changing technology also plays a role with sensor-based products giving way to the 'Internet of Things', which is made up of 'smart' devices, which have been connected to the web and become networks that share or gather data and information. This is all part of creating a more connected world. The lack of interoperability, that is, the inability of equipment or devices to operate in conjunction with each other, has also hampered progress. Even as this problem is tackled to make it cheaper and easier for devices to communicate and benefit from cross-product functionality, there still remains a lack of standards and protocols. There are numerous technical, operational and strategic hurdles yet to be overcome, not least around the very important topic of data security. There are likely to be a few more years of technology leap-frogging before *de facto* positions are found and maintained.

There remain many opportunities for technology to establish an important role in aiding us all as we age, and one could argue that we have time to play the long game as ageing populations are a worldwide trend. But there is a need for solutions now, particularly to better support the 'old-old' who have not grown up immersed in a digital and tech-based world. They too need to retain their freedom and autonomy as long as possible, while continuing to feel safe and secure both in and outside the home. But whilst there are unmet needs that technology could fill, there remain challenges built into this newly emerging sector with many older people and care professionals not always being early adopters.

In the following sections we look at technologies and innovations that can support and bolster relationships as well as those that could, if not used properly, lead to distancing or the loss of mutual respect or value. We will also look at some technologies that are already being deployed or tested and which of these have merits and so deserve to be more widely used. I hope you find this gallop through what is a wide-ranging and complex field insightful and interesting.

The current technology landscape for later life living

The ecosystem of businesses developing or offering products that help us as we age has largely formed under the blanket term of 'age tech'. Within this core category, several industry sub-categories have emerged: care tech, health tech, med tech and longevity tech. This chapter focusses on care tech and health tech as the most relevant aspects of relationships.

There are two sides to this technology landscape: the *supply side*, made up of businesses and organisations that have innovations which they are looking to develop and commercialise, and the *demand side*, which comprises consumers and organisations such as housing, health and care providers, Local Authorities and other local government organisations who want to identify, adopt and benefit from innovations. Together, these two sides make up what is known as the Silver Economy.

Since 2016, the EU-funded AgeTech Accelerator programme, mentioned earlier, has scouted for, identified and supported innovating businesses, helping them validate the needs of end-users, co-develop solutions and test their products and services with demand side actors across the four countries. More information about the programme can be found on the programme website along with a guide to entering the silver economy, a market study of the four countries and a route-to-market tool. A link to the programme website is given in the resources section at the end of this chapter.

The AgeTech Accelerator programme has identified and collected data on more than 900 innovative products which are categorised and cross-referenced by support domain (i.e., who they can benefit), target market and the level of dependency to which they are suited. This provides important intelligence on the agetech market as it stands now and as it develops and helps to identify where there is oversupply, where advances are needed, where there are trends and possibilities and the most likely routes to market.

There are several established incumbents in the market such as Astraline, EasyLink, Wel Being and Tunstall who have led the way in introducing technology such as telecare into home and formal care environments and that continue to evolve connected care. However, there has also been a proliferation of new technologies vying to find a sustainable business model and traction in the market. Two areas have already attracted a huge amount of interest from developers over the last few years and are not likely to see further significant advances. These are in the areas of digital communication and wellbeing tracking. Over 250 businesses on the AgeTech Accelerator database offer products with these two propositions, which indicates the level of competition in both these areas.

The following table shows product domains we have gathered data on so far (excluding telecare, care management systems, med tech and longevity tech) ranked from the most common themes to the least common target application for which they are being developed.

Product domain themes from most to least common

1. Communication	11. Medication reminders	22. Market place
2. Wellbeing tracking	12. Vital signs tracking	23. Finance
3. Memory care	13. Education and learning	24. Frailty assistance
4. Healthcare – virtual	14. Companion – virtual	25. Transportation modes
5. Falls alerts and prevention	15. Sense assist	26. Work in retirement
6. Social activities	16. Furniture and equipment for homes and clinical environments	27. Legacy
7. Mobility	17. Household assistance	28. Clothing (does not include wearables)
8. Exercise and fitness	18. Sleep	29. Continence
9. Robotics	19. Leisure activities and travel	30. End of life planning
10. Community participation	20. Security	31. Hygiene
	21. Eating and drinking	

Likewise, we can break down the products by target market, though several target multiple markets.

Products by target market from most to least targeted

1. Self-buyer	7. Nursing home	13. Physiotherapist
2. Carer – informal	8. Hospital	14. Occupational therapist
3. Care home	9. General Practitioner	15. Corporate/insurer
4. Care provider – formal	10. Housing association	16. Retirement developer
5. Dementia home	11. Smart home	17. Community association
6. Local Authority social care	12. Community nurse	18. Government

The range of technologies that are emerging covers a wide of applications, and many of them have behind them smart people and great motivations and intentions, yet few of these products are finding the market easy to access. So why is that?

There are several reasons: awareness, trust, complexity, shared values, pace of technological change. These will each be considered in turn.

Awareness

The digital world in which we live has made information both more accessible and less accessible. More accessible in terms of the breadth and depth of information that is available but less accessible in terms of central repositories of knowledge and information to which people are easily signposted. Platforms like Orcha, a health app evaluation and advisor organisation, provide an excellent service for health and social care professionals looking for accredited health apps, but consumers may well not be aware of it. The majority of product areas do not have such an emerging information hub, and so in a fragmented eco-system, many good products and applications get overlooked while less effective products get deployed.

Trust

Whilst older people cannot and should not be corralled into one homogeneous group and have as diverse a range of mindsets and motivation levels as younger generations, it is fair to say that anyone over the age of 50 has not grown up fully immersed in the digital world, so their perceptions and acceptance of new technologies, such as smart phones, can differ widely. So too does sharing information such as personal or health with anyone other than a health professional. What happens to data and how it is used is a concern for most people, and the increasing inter-connectivity of the world can make older people reticent about sharing information, while concern for its security remains a key issue.

Complexity

Many of the early tech products were not designed to reflect the way that bodies naturally change as people get older. Whilst there are upsides such as the need for less sleep, senses such as sight, hearing and touch decline, and this can impact on how easy products are to use and handle. But at the same time products need not be too simple. The term 'universal design' emerged as a concept for good design that made products accessible to all people regardless of age, disability or other factors.

Shared values

Many products designed with the good intention of keeping an older family member or loved one safe were met with resistance from the person who had to live with that technology in their home or on their person. Developing products in isolation from the target market meant that these products were not fit-for-purpose or were not a desirable solution. More and more businesses and developers recognise the value of co-creation and testing with their target markets, and programmes like the AgeTech Accelerator offer this service for both UK and overseas companies. But a full field test and pilot with validated outputs can be quite expensive for businesses, particularly start-ups or small businesses unless they are part of a funded programme such as SEAS 2Grow. Promisingly, though, much contemporary focus is on funding healthy ageing and later life living, and more programmes and funding competitions are being opened every week.

Pace of technological change

We are living in an age in which everything, including technology, changes rapidly. Whilst in some areas of business and society, the speed of that change offers benefits or opportunities, in the domain of age tech, it has meant that *de facto* platforms or systems have not yet emerged.

Combine these various constraints and suddenly it does not seem surprising that age tech is taking time to establish itself as an asset class in the way that fintech or proptech (digital advances in finance and property) have. However, with big tech giants such as Google, Amazon and Facebook eyeing the market and recognising the value of the 'silver dollar', great leaps have been made to overcome some of these constraints, with voice control and artificial intelligence simplifying technology interfaces and creating platforms that are accessible for everyone.

So, with that positive thought in mind, we can next look at some of the cutting-edge products and technologies that are available, before we turn to specific innovations for relational care.

Robotics

When people think about the future of care, they often think about robots. There is no shortage of examples of machines of differing levels of functionality and automation aiming at both the consumer and the business market. Most are currently at the research and concept stage, and there are still many conversations to be had about acceptability, but in my view in two decades time, some will have become a key part of most people's lives.

Care-O-Bot is a service robot developed by the Fraunhofer Institute for Manufacturing in Germany and designed for multiple environments, including the home and healthcare. Its fourth-generation concept has a modular design and has enhanced agility and 360 degree rotations of head and torso, which extends the robot's agility and working space.

Obi is a dining robot for people who lack upper limb function and which replicates the motion of a human arm during eating. The diner controls the food delivery using a switch mechanism tailored to the person, which selects the food from four different compartments on a specially designed plate before delivering it to the mouth.

Somnox is a soft bean-shaped sleep robot which can reduce stress and anxiety. It has a natural breathing rhythm and can play soothing sounds on demand. Designed to be used in bed at night time to promote and encourage a regular sleep pattern, it may also have application for helping instil calmness in some people during the daytime.

Atoun is a wearable robot for nursing and care workers and helps to reduce the amount of time required for a task and to lighten the strain on the body. Operating as an exo-skeleton and also known as 'powered wear', the wearable frame enhances personal levels of power and strength to help with tasks such as moving and lifting.

Moxi is a hospital robot assistant that helps clinical staff with non-patient-facing tasks like gathering supplies and bringing them to patient rooms, delivering lab samples, fetching items from central supply and removing soiled linen bags.

Stevie is a socially assistive robot designed for care homes. It can be pro-grammed to play games, make deliveries to residents and facilitate video chats.

Health diagnostics and hygiene

Another area which has potential and which meets specific needs, particularly for care and nursing home environments, is health diagnostics and hygiene. The following innovations are leading the way in terms of concepts.

Lifelight is a health monitoring app using a smart phone, which takes blood pressure, pulse and breathing rate readings in 40 seconds by a patient looking into a smart phone or tablet device.

Envision glasses are artificial intelligence-powered smart glasses designed to maintain independence in the blind or visually impaired and which read text from all kinds of surface in over 60 languages. The glasses can describe scenes, detect colours and scan barcodes.

HeardThat is an app that works with hearing devices to focus on a conver-sation by screening out background noise, allowing those with hearing impair-ment to converse normally in busy and noisy environments.

Abena Nova is an intelligent continence aid that uses built-in sensors to help caregivers provide personalised hygiene care.

TrueLoo is a smart toilet that can detect who is using it and that analyses waste for emerging conditions such as urinary tract infection, colitis and Type 2 diabetes.

Mobility

Another area that is seeing significant advances is mobility, and here are a few interesting concepts and ideas currently being tested and developed:

Zeen is a highly adaptable wheelchair which supports someone in everyday activities of living as well as more active interests such as sport.

Segway S-Pod prototype is a self-balancing two-wheeled electric wheel-chair with a navigation pad, designed for enclosed spaces such as large health care facilities or care homes with outside spaces or large gardens. It can go up to speeds of 24 miles per hour and has a current range of 43 miles.

Screwo Bro is a futuristic wheelchair which can tackle a wide range of ter-rains, including stairs.

Tek RMD is a mobility platform that allows a wheelchair user to move and stand independently and to navigate environments that a wheelchair would find less accessible.

Work in retirement, finance and end-of-life planning

And finally, we look some products that deal with the practicalities of the here and now such as work in retirement, finance and end-of-life planning. These are all areas which show potential for growth and impact.

Kalgera is a digital platform that securely collects financial data all in one place and that can send alerts if there are problems or unusual activity.

Pension Bee is a digital service which allows individuals to transfer their old pensions into one central and simplified pension plan.

Restless is a job notice board and community platform with details of jobs from age-friendly employers across the UK. It also provides information on distance learning courses, including those offering professional and business skills.

My Wishes is a digital service helping plan for end of life, which holds information such as a digital will, a goodbye message, funeral wishes and advance care planning as well as a Bucket List.

There are many hundreds, possibly thousands, of other products on the market that can help with later life living. The use of data to predict a fall before it happens is integrated into many wearable products as well as those designed for occupational and physiotherapists. There are also many ways to help and manage cognitive decline whether in the early or more advanced stages and so too for medication management, social and community communication, exercise and care management.

Many of the products specifically highlighted in this section are still at the concept or prototype stage, although some are fully developed and are already on the market. They have been chosen to represent areas where technology is advancing and that may offer the potential to help maintain quality of life, life purpose and a sense of value in the world as we get older. It will be very interesting to follow the more fledgling and cutting-edge ideas.

In the next section we return to the central theme of this book and look at how technologies can and do impact on relational care. But before that the reader may like to take a little light-hearted detour to look at the relationship between the older generation and the emerging class of digital assistants, to be found in the spoof advert for Amazon Echo Silver. The link to this advert, which is hosted on YouTube, can be found in the resources section at the end of this chapter – it is well worth taking a few minutes to enjoy it.

What technologies might specifically help with forming or maintaining human relationships?

What might this proliferation of technology mean for relational care? Are there types of products or categories that have potential to create an environment that favours personal, longer-term relationships? Are there types of individual products or categories that might be counter-productive? Or is this hard to gauge at this point?

As with all applications of technology or new ways of working, much of it depends on the human who is driving it. Good technologies can be bad in the wrong hands, and poorly designed technologies can still be helpful or have good impact in the right hands. In theory, within the many thousands of new products or services that have become available, there will be some that can truly contribute to helping relationships between care giver and receiver, whether that is in a formal care environment or within the family or informal care circle.

Much good work has already been done to try and understand how older people use technology or conversely why they do not use it. For example the *Technology and Older People Evidence Review* (Age UK, 2009), published in 2009 alongside the Digital Britain White Paper, provided good insights into the state of play at that time, though there has been significant progress in the last ten years, particularly in the way that the older population has embraced social media. The fastest growing group on Facebook, for example are those aged 65 and over, and in the UK the same applies to the take-up of some other digital media such as WhatsApp and Skype (though more modern digital app-based products such as Instagram appear to be used much less). SEHTA (South East Health Technologies Alliance) also published a useful review in 2016 of technology and innovation in Care Homes, and Keren Etkin, a gerontologist and tech enthusiast in Israel, publishes an annual age-tech market map (there is a link to market map for 2020 in the resources section).

There are two positions from which to address this question of why older people use technology – from the side of the person who is receiving help, support or care and from the side of the person who is giving it, who might be a family member, domiciliary care worker, social or health care professional. From each of these perspectives the benefits and disadvantages might be considered very differently.

One example of this is sensor-based systems that can be installed in people's homes to help build up a profile of someone's normal routines and activities and that, in the main, were designed by and ultimately bought by the middle-aged children of older adults rather than the older adults themselves. Children perceived this to be a caring and positive way of engaging with their parent because they were able to track the older person's wellbeing from a mobile phone and could be quickly alerted to problems that had happened or might happen. Most older people recoiled from this, seeing it instead as a form of surveillance or an invasion of their privacy. So, who is right? Both, of course.

Yet there are some good uses for this type of monitoring technology; for instance, there are examples of older couples where one person is still well and active, but the other has accelerating functional or cognitive decline. Installing sensors and even cameras can help one spouse retain some form of independence and continue normal activities of life while knowing that the other is safe, because they can see and can be alerted to any problems that might arise.

In this instance, intra-generational agreement seems to be more readily reached than cross-generational agreement. On the web there is a funny but insightful spoof video called 'Uninvited Guests' about the way a wily older man confounds the 'smart' products his children have put into his home to make sure he is eating healthily, sleeping at regular times and getting enough exercise. It is worth a few minutes to watch it, and the link can be found in the resources section at the end of this chapter.

The key point seems to be that technology can be a benefit if that older person feels that its adoption is something that is being done 'with' them and their consent, rather than 'to' them as an object rather than an involved human.

Earlier in this book we learned that relationships of all types (families, friends, carers) are critical to wellbeing and flourishing and that care provided to older people should be centred on promoting relationships rather than solely on the individual. The term 'relational' has been used to describe the phenomenon of a network of caring relationships, not centred on any single individual, but encouraging individual wellbeing and resilience. However, the term 'relational care' can also be used to describe care given by or within the family and supporting family involvement in long-term residential care. Ultimately at its heart resides the need for multidirectional relationships where the value of engagement is felt on all sides by all parties.

Taking that into consideration, how could technology help or support multidirectional relationships to thrive in different settings?

Connection and communication

There is no shortage of products that allow people to connect and communicate remotely and that are available often at no cost for the basic service. These are usually digital platforms or apps and began with products like Skype and Webex being available on personal computers. But in the last few years, these products have become mobile and have been joined by platforms like Zoom, OneClick-Chat, GoogleMeetup and Houseparty. As these products are now ubiquitous and more and more older people are using them, there is no need to consider them in detail here; there are links to their websites in the resources section.

Another category of products that have become popular over the last few years are those that connect older people to potential new friends and social circles. These products, such as Buddy Hub, which is an online platform or face-to-face befriending services, such as those run by the Royal Voluntary Services, appeal to some older people. Schemes like the one that Communicare run on the south coast offer social events such as lunch clubs and encourage regular attendance. Lifeloop is a product for enhancing resident and family engagement in retirement communities; whilst this type of product is good at managing and encouraging social interactions and engagement between the family and community, they do operate at the mechanistic level rather than the humanistic level. Therefore, developing or improving relationships is more of a side effect than an intrinsic part of the design.

Gransnet is a useful and popular forum, with advice and support on a wide range of topics, and offers forums, a virtual book club, life hacks and advice on style and beauty for the older woman. There is lots of activity on the site, but less evidence about the relationships that are formed or developed.

Does this mean that there are no technology products designed specifically with relationship support in mind? Or do we just need to look at them differently or perhaps use them in a different way? If relationships are formed and maintained through shared or lived experiences and are based on mutual respect, trust and acceptance, might there perhaps be products or ideas that might support these feelings?

Replicating and sharing experience

Approaching this from the point of view of mutual understanding and knowledge, perhaps the first thing could be for younger people to understand better what it is like to get old. As part of the lived experience, stepping into the shoes of an older person and experiencing the impact of functional and cognitive decline might be the first time that someone begins to empathise with someone in their care. A product called GERT, which stands for Gerontologic Simulator Suite, has been developed and has been used by Barclays Bank to help sensitise their employees to how and why older people might find doing some tasks more difficult. There is a short video on YouTube that shows what the experience of using this is like (link to be found in resources).

Once someone begins to understand and appreciate the physical effects of ageing, the next stage in developing foundations for a relationship might be to learn about someone's life and to evolve from seeing them from an objective view of 'an older person' to a subjective view of 'gran' or 'Margaret who was a ballet dancer when she was young and ran away to get married'. Products such as Remarkable Lives and Kindeo help bring together personal and family stories along with photos and video to create a digital archive of memories that can be shared with family, friends and carers. Creating and sharing this kind of legacy should help maintain a sense of self for someone as an important and valuable individual. This will be particularly true if the gathering of material is a joint enterprise between an older person and a relative or carer, as mutual knowledge will be developed during the process. Yet only a few of these products find a viable business model, and they seem not to be gaining the traction they deserve. One wonders if this might be because building relationships in this way is not seen as the priority that it should be.

But what about sharing contemporary experiences or creating experiences in real time together? There are a wide range of products that allow for this. Games generated by products like Tovertafel or Omi are interesting and exciting for all generations and are particularly good for connecting with those in care who might be suffering from cognitive decline.

'It (Tovertafel) ensures that my Mum and I do more active things. Nothing can go wrong in the games; it's simply loads of fun! That motivates her to keep playing' (informal carer, cited on Tovertafel website).

Virtual reality is another concept that has been attractive to the later life market, with products like The Astonishing Visit, which allows a group of people to access the same VR space where they can virtually travel the world and discuss what they are seeing or experiencing. Similarly, The Way Back has vintage films and news from the past, which can be used to stimulate conversation and evoke happy feelings.

> 'It's so helpful for staff, carers.... And even family to have a tool like this to start a conversation. Sometimes that can be the hardest thing' (manager, community project, cited on the Way Back website).

Shared experiences can be active too. Some of the products that enable these experiences are supported by background technology that provides the means to the end. One example is the social enterprise Dementia Adventure, which offers supported holidays and adventures for people living with dementia and their loved ones to enjoy together, illustrating that cognitive decline does not have to be as restrictive as we sometimes think. It uses technology to exchange information and create a sense of community, sharing and learning from each other so that better care can be given. Another example is Element 3 Health, a membership network of activity clubs that gets members active physically, socially and mentally. People with shared interests are matched and kept in contact with like-minded people, which helps overcome the anxiety or shyness that some people might feel when they are meeting new people or joining new activities.

Interactive robotics

But what role can technology play in relational care for people who have higher dependency levels or are confined to a care or nursing home, as in the last few years of life, relationships are more important than ever? Particularly where those relationships might need to be developed with people who are not family or friends but formal carers who might change regularly and who will often be looking after people with complex health issues?

Innovations that can help to alleviate anxiety and agitation among residents, allowing for more relaxed contact and readiness to accept interaction with carers, are being trialled in some care homes. Robotic animals powered by artificial intelligence are being used, often made in the image of a pet. But not always. Some are designed to perform tricks, but all are designed to pull at the heart strings. For some people surprisingly strong bonds appear to be created with them, even when they know they are not real. These robo-animals range from the expensive to the cost-effective. From the imaginative to the realistic.

Some, for example a small futuristic looking puppy, may retail at a high price. But products which look and move like small dogs can be bought from places such as Amazon or eBay at a fraction of the cost and appear to generate responses that are just as positive, even if they do not have all the attributes of a real dog.

'We bought some blue dogs whose eyes moved and they barked. They were blue and white toys made for children but in some residents we saw a reduction in distress and anxiety. To them the colour didn't matter. We saw as much response from that £20 investment as one home that bought a product at £4000' (care home manager).

The advanced interactive robots that sell for thousands of pounds can perceive people and their environment, will respond to their names and are based on a much more sophisticated technology. Even so, if the response generated is similar and finances are not available, there is a big saving between those and the toy dog.

Doll therapy, which also uses increasingly lifelike dolls to help calm those with later stages of dementia, is now a recognised approach. It has been shown to help a person sleep and can create a positive distraction, which allows for normal dialogue between a person and their carer. However, the approach remains controversial. An article in *The Guardian* ('Lifelike Dolls in Dementia Care', 22.1.20) looks at both sides of the debate. On the one hand, advocates of the approach argue that particularly for those in the middle or later stages of dementia, it can give reassurance, leading to a greater level of engagement and calmness, more so than other approaches that have been tried. But on the other hand, there are families who feel uncomfortable seeing their older loved ones with dolls, and some professionals believe it takes away a person's dignity and involves treating them like a child. There are other issues such as doll logistics – how to present the doll to the person, what happens if it gets broken and how to deal with unexpected consequences like someone with dementia getting distressed because they think their doll baby has died when its eyes have closed. This debate about the value of these types of products and whether ethically they are acceptable will no doubt continue. Here are two points of view from care home workers:

'I'm particularly interested in terms of relationships – if someone with advanced dementia is cuddling a robot cat or blue dog, does that distract them from relating to people like a pacifier for a child or does it help them relate, therefore, they are calmer?'

'The only thing I have witnessed is the extra communication. That person is using it to show others, to engage, to say what she and her cat have been doing. It's aided communication and engagement with others.'

Music-based technology

The use of music as a way of helping to reduce anxiety and distress is another area which has seen increasing focus over the last few years, with products such as Memory Tracks indicating that by song-task association, they can support important daily routines. It connects reminiscence songs to necessary tasks, and evidence suggests that over time, it can change behaviour and make it much easier to give and receive care. A very interesting approach is also offered by a Dutch company called CRDL, which has developed a care instrument made of wood that uses intelligent software to translate physical contact between people into sound. CRDL can help overcome some of the difficulties associated with caring for people who may become very withdrawn and who may not want to be touched. A quote from the website:

> 'It is moving to see how the clients react to it. You experience a real means of being able to make contact using music and sounds. Using CRDL doesn't only affect the clients, but also their family and carers. It is a beautiful moment when you can get people out of their isolation' (specialised carer and housing supervisor).

Can technology assist relationships?

Over the course of this section, we have been looking at how technology might help relationships and have considered how communication and tasks could be improved by using particular types of product. Yet as proposed at the beginning of this section, in the wrong hands or even unintentionally, applying a technological solution can or might hinder relationships.

To take three examples: some advanced technologies such as virtual reality can produce benefits by bringing people together into a shared experience, but equally they have the potential to disorientate some older people, particularly those with cognitive issues; and often the headsets are considered too heavy or cumbersome and the service too expensive. The use of robotic animals or dolls does calm and re-focus some people with dementia, but on the other hand, they are seen by some researchers and those involved in safeguarding vulnerable people as tricking them into 'deceitful' relationships. Schemes or online platforms that serve to connect older people with new companions or helpers need to be carefully managed to make sure that volunteers are properly checked and that transactions or connections are transparent and safe.

And finally, there is the need to be mindful that technologies should be there to assist and not to replace, to enhance and not to pacify. And that responsibility lies with all of us.

Summary and lessons learned

The technologies covered in this chapter are not exhaustive. Far from it. Every day new ideas and concepts are developed, and more and more products for later life living and healthy ageing come to the market.

Whilst services such as telecare have been around for a long time, many new products have been developed over the last five years as digital and mobile technologies have advanced. Many of these have not been readily accepted by the older generation although, at the time this book is being written in the Spring of 2020, the outbreak of Covid-19 is forcing the adoption of products and platforms for digital communication, to help older people who are confined to home as a protection against the novel Coronavirus.

In some categories of product where there is an oversupply and where competition is fierce, few products are finding commercial models that allow for scaling up, nor are they attracting the interest of investors. Other categories cry out for more solutions, such as cleanliness and hygiene, food and drink, transportation and end-of life-planning. These are the areas where opportunities lie. Two key factors seem to be impacting the growth and mass adoption of new products: firstly, awareness and where to find them, secondly, how to ensure there is shared value between those using or introducing technology and those that are impacted by it or the object of its delivery.

So is technology the friend or foe of relational care? On balance, it is set to make a positive contribution to health and social care, but with the caveat that it needs to be in the right hands and to be used with the right intentions. Let's look at ways that technology can impact relationships and what can be learnt.

Evidenced and potential impacts

- The right technology in the right hands can enhance relationships particularly in formal care settings
- Products that encourage shared experiences can help with forming relationships even in later life or in formal care settings
- Several emerging therapies, such as doll therapy and robot-animal therapy, remain controversial, but there is increasing interest in and proof of their efficacy
- Products with the most impact are generally those that have been developed in collaboration with the groups of people that will use or benefit from them

Learning points

- There is no shortage of products aimed at independent living or the care sector, but some categories are in oversupply, while some key areas require more focus and more solutions
- Technologies will need to be embraced in order to help maintain quality of life and wellness as people age

- The pace of technological change means that few established approaches are emerging
- Products are adopted and actively sought out when they offer value to all parties involved in or impacted by their use
- Some technologies, such as virtual reality or those that involve putting devices on or around the face, have to be carefully introduced as older people or those suffering from dementia can find these distressing
- Many older people or their families are not aware of or cannot find the products that will help them
- As technology advances, concepts such as robotics will increasingly support care and health workers but are unlikely to replace them

Links to resources

Amazon Echo Silver https://www.youtube.com/watch?v=YvT_gqs5ETk

'Barclays Bank uses the GERT suit to help educate their employees to the realities of ageing': http://www.age-simulation-suit.com/barclays.html (accessed March 2020).

Gerontologist, The – 2020 Age Tech Market Map – https://www.thegerontechnologist.com/

Innovation and Technology in Care Homes (2016), The SEHTA Review. https://www.sehta.co.uk/cms-data/depot/sehta/Technology-Innovation-in-Care-Homes-The-SEHTA-Review.pdf.

'Lifelike dolls in dementia care' 2020, *The Guardian:* https://www.theguardian.com/society/2020/jan/22/lifelike-dolls-dementia-care

Royal Voluntary Service: https://www.royalvoluntaryservice.org.uk/our-services/supporting-people/community-companions?gclid=EAIaIQobChMIterK-u3J6AIVWpnVCh1C2wyzEAAYBCAAEgKf5PD_BwE

Tech Crunch: https://techcrunch.com/

Technology and Older People Evidence Review, 2009, Age UK: https://www.ageuk.org.uk/Documents/EN-GB/For-professionals/Research/Evidence_Review_Technology.pdf?dtrk=true (accessed March 2020)

Uninvited Guests video: https://vimeo.com/128873380 (accessed March 2020)

Links to products mentioned in this chapter

Abena Nova: http://www.abenanova.com/

Aibo Robot Dog: https://us.aibo.com/

Arjo: https://www.arjo.com/int/products/medical-beds/wellness

Atoun: https://news.panasonic.com/global/topics/2019/70659.html

Buddy hub: https://www.buddyhub.co.uk/

Care-O-bot: https://www.care-o-bot.de/en/care-o-bot-4.html

Dementia Adventure: https://dementiaadventure.co.uk/

Element3Health: https://element3health.com/products/

Envision: https://www.letsenvision.com/glasses

GERT: http://www.age-simulation-suit.com/?gclid=CjwKCAjwguzzBRBiEiwAgU0FT8mMuocaHn3Ok1iBEpSyUJALdP5UjmcicfppX535s0yBnO_QIRWOKxoC-qB4QAvD_BwE

HeardThat: https://heardthatapp.com/

House Party: https://houseparty.com/
Kalgera: https://kalgera.com/
Kindeo: http://www.age-simulation-suit.com/barclays.html
Lifelight: https://lifelight.ai/
LifeLoop: https://ourlifeloop.com/
Memory Tracks: https://www.memorytracks.co.uk/
Moxi: https://diligentrobots.com/moxi/
My Wishes: https://www.mywishes.co.uk/
Obi dining robot: https://meetobi.com/
OneClickChat: https://oneclick.chat/#adults
Oomph Wellness: https://www.oomph-wellness.org/
Orcha: https://www.orcha.co.uk/who-we-help/health-and-care/
Omi: https://omi.uk/
Paro: http://www.parorobots.com/
Pension Bee: https://www.pensionbee.com/
Remarkable Lives: https://remarkablelives.co.uk/
ReminisCence: https://www.reminiscence.co.uk/about-us
Restless: https://restless.co.uk/
Screwo bro: https://screwo.ch/en/bro/
Segway S-Pod: https://interestingengineering.com/video/the-s-pod-segways-self-balancing-electric-wheelchair-inspired-by-jurassic-world
Somnox: https://meetsomnox.com/
Sony: https://us.aibo.com/
Stevie: www.stevietherobot.com
Tek RMD: https://matiarobotics.com/
TrueLoo: www.toilabs.com
Tovertafel https://tovertafel.co.uk
Way Back, The: https://thewaybackvr.com/
Zeen: https://www.exokinetics.com/

6

THE FUTURE OF RELATIONAL CARE

Relational care and critical change

The lived experiences of older people, their carers and the managers of care delivery projects – heard through their own voices as well as evidenced by research – argue strongly for a sea change in attitudes and policy to enable flourishing, with more contentment and fulfilment for all involved in the process of ageing. It can be achieved through changes in ethos, practice and investment priorities, but this begs the question of the viability of concomitant changes needed in policy and finance. Can the costs and benefits be measured and how challenging are new ways of doing things?

Over much of history, living to a good old age surrounded by one's family was a rare privilege and sought-after ambition, reserved for the lucky few. Recent scientific and medical advances have now brought this possibility to the majority of people in developed countries, yet the gift of old age risks being seen as a poisoned chalice for individuals and society. Far from the aged being the blessed ones, their presence now risks being calculated in terms of a burden and expenditure. Yet they are not 'the other', they are our present or future selves and as we have seen in previous chapters, they are a valuable part of society right now.

The tendency to 'other' older people is expressed both in the subtle attitudes embedded in matters of policy and funding and the overt prejudice to be found daily on social media and in casual conversation. This results not only in unnecessary division between generations, but also within the older generation, as Mowat and Mowat warn: 'Social policy can easily have the effect of splitting older people into different camps, and thereby can reduce the power of any … coherent rational voice …. We need to live with each other in a state of mutual recognition of our common humanity' (2018, p. 115). Lodge et al. (2016) conclude that 'official responses to increased longevity represent a social policy failure' (Barnes et al., 2018, p. 12).

This tendency leads to ageism, a basic discomfort with the idea of one's own ageing and with the living evidence of older people as a reminder of mortality. There is a trajectory towards a general dislike of age that has been employed by policy makers to their own ends: 'The negative framing of population ageing as a burden on resources has been evident for some time, [but] there is evidence that this has intensified as governments increasingly mobilise population ageing to justify responses to the economic recession' (Barnes et al., 2018, p. 20).

As Storlie summarises: 'Ageism is a dehumanizing and demoralizing cross-cultural social problem' (2015 p. xx), and indeed while the worst excesses of ageism express themselves as elder abuse, it can be subtly invasive, 'out of fear and loathing for mortality, we will not acknowledge them [elders] as our own, as extended versions of us all' (Koch, 2000, p. 172); they are 'frustrating and vexing challenges to the model of adulthood that society holds dear' (ibid., p. ix).

The roots of ageism can be traced back to a number of philosophies and attitudes that gained ground in the nineteenth and twentieth centuries, including the discounting of older people as no longer of developmental interest by Sigmund Freud and the growth of utilitarianism: 'a cultural emphasis on utilitarian economic concerns … [emphasises] … issues of financial burden and cost-efficient care' (ibid., p. 9). Koch describes the lives of a wide variety of older people through listening to and reflecting on their own voices and concludes: 'ageism's simplistic assumptions – age equals cost without benefit; youth equals utility – are as baseless as they are generally accepted' (ibid., p. 8). He talks of 'the assumption – utilitarian and exact – …that youth is more valuable than seniority. Seniors are expensive' (ibid., p. 7).

However, the challenge to these assumptions must come in part from envisaging viable alternatives on which new policy can be based rather than simply rejecting them as inhumane. In *Re-imagining Old Age*, Barnes et al. not only challenge the dominance of 'the individualistic assumption of neoliberalism' but argue, as indeed this book strongly does, that 'the basis for justice and wellbeing lies in our fundamental interdependence' (2018, p. 188). This is a matter both of justice, which should be 'central to decision-making about social and health-care policies' (Mowat and Mowat, 2018, p. 64), and also of common sense about human relationships as the basis of a stable society. 'Lack of trust in relationships raises anxiety and is a big [social] problem' (ibid., p. 128).

The previous chapters have aimed to put forward evidence for the value of relational care in promoting wellbeing, happier and more fulfilled lives where all individuals matter – as Koch says, 'An older adult, once objectified, can more easily be denied rights and opportunities' (2000, p. 77) – but this does not negate the need to be realistic about what can be done differently.

How can benefits be measured?

The challenges of measuring wellbeing

Common sense alone is rarely enough to engender change, as those who have the power to make things happen in ways that are different to the recent past are likely be held to account by public opinion and specialist advisors. They need to have grounds for their decisions. It is therefore worth considering whether any meaningful measurements can be applied to the apparent benefits of shifting care in the direction of a new paradigm based on relationships and interdependence. Different measuring tools and models are discussed in detail in Appendix A, and the section that follows here is concerned with the general challenges of measurement as they relate to decisions about policy and practice.

There are undeniably problems with measuring wellbeing, a concept which in itself often needs clearer definition; as Barnes et al point out, this must be recognised as 'a subjective state' (2018, p. 128) that cannot be assessed in the way that material wealth can be but must be 'experienced'. Therefore, measurement is highly reliant on self-reporting in terms of feelings such as satisfaction or anxiety, which are in turn affected by matters like self-awareness, insight and memory. Cromby advises that where wellbeing questionnaires or interviews are concerned 'their reliability and validity might be better accounted for as products of their ability to model, rather than measure, psychological processes' (2011, p. 840). Additionally, participating in such surveys can affect mood, if they draw the subject's awareness to their own negative feelings. So perhaps it is those who are giving, rather than receiving, care who should be consulted on wellbeing levels? Yet Feinstein, writing in Cluff and Binstock (2001, p. 208), comments that 'caring (rather than curing) … cannot be evaluated by [its] providers' but must either be by 'direct observation and monitoring or must rely on retrospective enquiry from its recipients' which amounts to 'subjective reports'.

The arguments might seem to be circular, and this is in part because we are accustomed to measuring so much in terms of targets, outcomes and outputs. As Horesh says, numerical targets are at their worst, the 'outgrowths of gesture politics' (2008, p. 18), and sometimes they just seem to be plucked out of thin air; they are also narrow, where they should be 'inextricably linked to wellbeing' (ibid., p. 63). 'Socially beneficial outcomes' (ibid., p. 20) rarely drive government policy and, influenced by factors beyond the control of those who set them, any outcome (beneficial or otherwise) does not often lead to its instigator taking responsibility for it. Horesh argues for a particular system (Social Policy Bonds) that would see outcomes rather than activities valued in the delivery of government plans. This might be a useful way to approach care provision for older people, although it would also be important to take account of the ways in which the outcomes were achieved, as some may have more positive incidental effects than others.

Questions of measurement are fraught with difficulty in the case of human flourishing, yet most of us feel we can recognise its presence or absence. New ways of approaching the challenge are described shortly, but first, it is important to acknowledge that all human beings are valuable, whatever their age. The type of ageism described above can start to erode the perceived value of older people, such that any form of measurement is based on an assumption that the older the person, the less they are 'worth'. Woodward's book *Valuing Age* (2008), referred to in previous chapters, tackles and explores this assumption head-on, as he asks us to consider, what is the point of older people?

Value of older people

As we have seen, age is frequently problematised, both for the individual and society. People become 'burdens', not only in terms of social policy but in their own minds, and their role in the community goes unrecognised. This is exacerbated by the recent reappraisal of the 'third age' as one during which people are still active, and the creation of a new a 'fourth age' of frail dependency, which, as Barnes et al. say, 'does nothing to challenge the negative stereotyping associated with dependence and burden' (2018, p. 17) but simply shifts it to a later age. Negativity attaches to concepts of need and non-contribution: but this is on the basis of a narrow definition of contribution associated with economic activity or donation of time to providing assistance such as childcare, voluntary work in the community and so on. It does not encompass the real nature of the value that a much older person can still bring to society if they are enabled to remain engaged.

The World Health Organisation envisages a broader definition of 'active ageing' that includes 'frail and disabled people' who nevertheless participate according to their 'needs, desires and capabilities' (WHO, 2002, p. 12). This wider approach challenges the idea of 'successful ageing', which is predicated on minimising disease and disability; high levels of physical and cognitive functioning; and the ability to remain actively engaged. The phrase implies that any falling short in these respects is 'unsuccessful' and thereby renders the 'failing' person less valuable. An overly rigid definition of 'successful ageing' risks impoverishing society by denying it the contribution that older people can reasonably make, and not investing in their engagement.

Participation in community both supports people and helps them in the search for life meaning, which, as we have seen, is more likely to be achieved in an environment of relational care.

> Today, the crisis of old age appears to be a crisis of meaning. Why am I still alive as a frail older person? …. What is the point of my life? Why do I have to continue to live when I am no longer accepted in our society?
>
> *(Missinne writing in Jewell, 2004, p. 111)*

If society takes a new look at how it can benefit from recognising the value of all humans, irrespective of age, and its ageing members can be acknowledged as bringing the gifts not only of their time but also of lessons learnt over years of living, then intergenerational misunderstandings and conflicts may be reduced and life enriched.

Those able to give active time may do so to 'teach remedial reading … [be] unpaid baby-sitters for grandchildren, and unpaid home carpenters and cooks for their own, adult children... that they are unpaid does not mean seniors are an inconsequential resource' (Koch, 2000, p. 155). But such activity is not the only type that should be valued; older people also bring time 'to reflect' (Goldsmith in Jewell, 2004, p. 38) and to share their lived experience. They are the only people who know first-hand what it actually feels like to be old; they bring 'a form of wisdom not only associated with the cumulative effect of knowledge ... but also the development of subtle skills honed through experience' (Barnes et al., 2018, p. 46). This is a form of mature spirituality explored earlier in Chapter 1, yet the irony is that nowadays Western society associates age not with knowledge and spiritual growth but with cognitive decline. 'Less than a century ago, age and its perspective were a sought after, honoured state' (Koch, 2000, p. 3) when 'we believed longevity led to wisdom' (ibid., p. 15).

'What value do we assign to old age?' (Jewell, 2004, p. 126). This is the critical challenge that needs to be met as part of measuring wellbeing and the factors which promote it. For if measurements are based primarily on physical health and the ability to contribute active time, frail older people will be assigned little value, failing to reflect the wider richness of a life well lived and the benefits of sharing this with others through meaningful relationships.

New approaches to measuring

Previous chapters have alluded to more innovative approaches to measurement, based not on targets and outputs but on feelings and support for the whole person. While recognising that feelings are by their nature subjective and transient, they are nevertheless real, with real-life consequences, and their effect cannot be underestimated. If relational care is to become the norm, then accepted ways of assessing its impact are required. Various measurement tools are examined in Appendix A, in the context of how they might be applied to relational care.

The Senses Framework – published in 2006 by Nolan et al., which represented a breakthrough in its recognition that any basis for assessment must 'start from the perspectives of older people themselves' (2006, p. 16) and 'see what older people themselves considered important' (ibid., p. 18) – makes a detailed argument for a qualitative approach and identifies the factors affecting perceptions of care.

Nolan et al. say: 'We believe that the Senses Framework has the potential to more fully articulate the conditions necessary to create and sustain "enriched environments" of care' (ibid., p. 123) and believes that judged by the criteria of perspective, practical approaches and taking into account all relevant knowledge, it has 'relevance far beyond nursing' (ibid., p. 127). He concludes: 'However, to realise its full potential the Framework needs to be considered alongside a relationship-centred, as opposed to a person-centred approach' (ibid., p. 130), which suggests that it could be used as part of a foundation for assessing the impacts of relational care in such a way as to make a case for policy change. Similarly, the Butterfly Model prioritises feelings over dictating behaviours, enabling staff to be more flexible in terms of allocating their time and being alongside those with dementia.

Insofar as residential care is concerned, other innovative measurement ideas have been put in place and found useful but are currently only applicable to residential settings. These include Hallmark's Thomas Tool and the Your Care Home survey by Ipsos MORI, both described in Appendix A. In common with the two models above, they take into consideration the feelings, perceptions and viewpoints not only of older people but also of carers and family and may therefore lend themselves to adaptation for wider use.

Any form of measurement that does not start by setting targets and recognising soft outcomes rather than hard outputs – in other words, the type of measurement likely to be suitable for use in relational care situations – will rely on changes in attitude and policy if it is to be considered valid by policy makers. The choices for those involved in care are to accept targets that are not in themselves unworthy, such as a reduction in falls, and also accept that these can be achieved irrespective of happiness or distress; to argue for a different philosophy of assessment based on listening and accepting what matters to older people and their carers; or to develop new 'soft' tools that enable the changes required for good relational care to be correlated to direct and indirect expenditure and cost savings.

Can the costs of relational care be assessed?

While older people should not and cannot be commoditised, nevertheless any service provision entails private or public money, and before addressing the policy implications of relational care, this chapter briefly considers issues of funding.

Funding models for purchase of services

Funding the provision of age care in the UK presents a complex picture, as public resources for adult social care are held by Local Authorities, coming partly from local sources such as business and domestic rates and partly from central government. As such, they are subject to both local and national policy as well as to individual means testing. The most recent forecast (2016) from the King's Fund and the Nuffield Trust is for a £1.9billion funding gap for social care, with more pressure on older people to find and pay for their own care (Barnes et al., 2018, p. 178). As at 2017, 41% residents in care homes funded themselves, 49% were receiving some Local Authority funding (25% of these were paying for some proportion of their own care) and the remaining 10% were receiving NHS funding for nursing care services.

To meet statutory requirements, a higher proportion of Local Authority (LA) budgets is being directed towards social care, the growing cost of which the Institute for Fiscal Studies believes has forced councils to reduce spending on all other services by 40% (report in **i** newspaper, 23.11.19). In London, for example, the real cost of provision per week for a residential place is about twice what most LAs pay, which is about £500 to £600. In Yorkshire an LA will pay a similar amount, but the cost of provision may be more like £800. So top-ups and private payments are essential and will vary greatly across the country.

Resources may also come from charities and philanthropists, either as donations to non-profit ventures or as owners and managers of services to which any excess income is returned for the purposes of improvement or client support.

Public funding for health care comes via the National Health Service, free at the point of delivery. Once the NHS takes over the entire payment, it can become viable, depending on the NHS band. But there are a number of blurred lines between health and social care, and hence between funding sources. Further, a significant proportion of community and residential provision is paid for privately by older people or their families, either as 'top-ups' or in full. It seems likely, given the Health Foundation poll cited below, that much of the resentment about private payment may stem from the opacity of the system, and its perceived unfairness.

The perception of the public cost of meeting the needs of an ageing population may fuel the severe ageism described in other chapters, yet in common with all funding issues is likely to be more complex in reality. For example, poor or inadequate care can impact the overall economy more than good provision would have done: data from the Centre for Economics and Business Research for the Alzheimer's Society show that businesses in England lost £3.2 billion in 2018 based on lost productivity from carers who have had to leave jobs or change working patterns to meet the needs of loved ones (report in a newspaper 28.9.11). Ethical owners of care providers and homes are faced with impossible dilemmas: 'I need to ensure the home is financially viable to meet the needs of the residents. Would I cut back in any areas and reduce quality? Absolutely not' (owner/director).

The phenomenon of 'bedblocking' or 'discharge culture' (Nolan et al., 2006, p. 106) in the NHS represents a cost to the system and a brake on its throughput and could also be another contributor to ageism. Watson cites the figure of £820 million spent by the NHS 'on keeping older patients in hospital when they no longer need acute treatment' (2018, p. 281). Nurses end up undertaking the tasks that could better be provided by carers in a long-term facility, or old people are sent home too early and 'bounce back to hospital in an even worse condition' (ibid., p. 282).

'One man, prior to admission, had nine emergency ambulances in one week. A phenomenal cost to the NHS. After moving in and getting the right care, he has had no more falls or hospital admissions' (home manager). Good care in nursing care homes or other residential facilities would cost the public purse far less, and it is not the fault of older people if such care does not exist in sufficient quantity.

Being old is not in itself necessarily an expensive condition; 'the equation – age equals costly, dependent fragility – is a scapegoat; in other words, a way in which blame for systemic failures of the health care system can be assigned easily if not reasonably to a single population'. While this comment was written about the US system (Koch, 2000, p. 155), the sentiments could equally be broadly applied to the UK. Some of our high costs are associated with poor or inappropriate care and policy based on outdated assumptions, misunderstandings or weight of perceived public opinion: a policy that changes with governments and ministers rather than on evidence. Other high costs are due to the way that care is delivered, which ranges from the excellent to the inhuman. The public purse could perhaps be saved some money, or at the very least, a great many older people and their carers could be happier and more settled, if policy were bolder, more compassionate and quicker to recognise what measurements are and are not suited to the wellbeing of humans.

The truth is that the UK population is not unreasonable, nor uncaring, nor unwilling to pay its way. The question is how payment should work, and whether it should be on the NHS model of general taxation. A survey conducted by Ipsos MORI on behalf of the Health Foundation (5 December 2019) shows increasing public support for paying more tax to maintain and improve health and social care: 62% of respondents, up from 51% in 2018. As far as social care is concerned, it is not the actual paying via the tax system but perceived unfairness in that system that is a problem: 46% felt means-testing was unfair (as opposed to 37% who found it acceptable) and 62% of people find it unacceptable to have to use the value of one's home to pay for care (as opposed to 21% answering 'acceptable').

The press summary for the report concludes:

> People are clearly now recognising the deep unfairness in how social care support for older people works and are increasingly dissatisfied. In stark contrast to the NHS, publicly funded social care is only provided free to those with the greatest need and the lowest means, leaving too many others no choice but to sell their homes to pay for care. The public is strongly against this – which is yet another warning that the issue can no longer be dodged. A new government should do the right thing and act fast.
>
> *(Ibid., p. 3)*

This conclusion is heartening given that writing only a year or so earlier, Barnes et al. were forced to conclude that 'There is little evidence that a sense of collective responsibility for care will prevail …. We seem to be moving away from a just society that recognises dependency as integral to the human condition' (2018, p. 179). As I write in 2020, the government has not acted, and which of these prognoses eventually will prevail will depend on factors including the economy, any sense of the re-integration of society and an acceptance of the benefits for everyone of improved care.

Opacity across the funding system affects not only care recipients but also providers. For example, a residential care home cannot be sustainable if all its residents are LA funded, as most LAs are unable to cover the full costs of a placement, even in a not-for-profit home. The 'care hours' an LA allocates to an individual living at home are rarely going to be sufficient for all physical needs to be met with dignity and thought, let alone emotional and social needs. As far as private recipients and residents 'subsidising' state ones, one care home manager called this 'ugly, and a complete mess that families find very difficult'. The financial director of another care home group explained to me:

> There is a middle ground where the care can be delivered at a very high quality and the residents needs can be met which doesn't have to be at very luxurious level but it's certainly higher than what the local authority is willing to pay. There's a difference between keeping people alive and keeping people meaningfully engaged. That's the difference. At £550 a week [the likely sort of LA funding rate], you can keep people alive but there's no budget there to do those extra things, for that extra time which is really required.

The LA will financially assess each funded individual and start to provide 'top-ups' once their assets fall below a certain level; this was described as 'painful' and 'unsustainable' by one manager. Where there is a condition such as dementia with high support needs, the care home must take the initiative with the LA and argue the case for more funding, which demands strong negotiation skills on the part of the individual manager. Some demanding physical or mental conditions may be covered by additional health funding, but others such as aggression are not.

Whatever the nature of the housing, the variable costs will be those pertaining to the service charge element, as the rent will be a fixed rate reflecting the locality. Many components of the service charge such as heating or food cannot be varied significantly, so the variable is really in the staffing costs, but an attempt to reduce this will affect the quality of care and relationships, setting aside any ethical issues.

Funding models for delivery of services

Who pays, at what point and how the costs are spread through society, all affect the nature of the care that can be delivered. Describing the convoluted payment coding systems in the United States, Cluff and Binstock explain how this 'procedural reductionism' has become so 'elaborate' that it leads to little gain (2001, p. 116) and can dominate decisions about the type of care service required. In that scenario, cost savings must be made by eliminating some services; paying less for them; or cutting the time allotted to them, each of which 'has a direct negative impact on the ability or the motivation to care' (ibid.).

Underfunding and complexity of funding impact on all types of community and residential support for older people; at the worst they lead to closures of schemes that people have come to call their home, with potentially disastrous human suffering.

> Factors which owners of closed private and voluntary homes feel contributed to their closure include low levels of fees paid by publicly funded residents, the cost implications of the national minimum standards, ... increases in running costs such as wages, the expectation that future local authority fees would not cover costs and problems with recruitment and retention of staff. .... Where a single cause was identified it was usually related to the low level of local authority fees.
>
> *(Help the Aged, 2007, p. 22)*

Even if closure is avoided, the very services that most support relational care may come under threat. In 2019, the largest social landlord in the UK, Clarion Housing Group, decided it could not afford the subsidy costs of providing a daily hot lunch to its residents in sheltered accommodation. Residents were reported to be devastated, saying, 'Going to lunch is the only time we can all sit at tables and chat to each other.' 'It's the daily meal that we all look forward to' (see report by Paul Gallagher, i newspaper, 25.1.20). Such erosions of daily life diminish wellbeing and resilience and lead to greater isolation, such that changes to health go less noticed until medical care is sought. This observation is not intended to be a criticism of struggling LAs, but to underline the subsequent higher costs of short-term cost savings, and the importance of a 'National Social Care Service' equivalent to the NHS that those polled in 2019 by the Health Foundation were calling for.

The NHS is by no means perfect, but it is valued as being largely fair in its delivery, based on need rather than ability to pay, and on the principle of funding through general taxation according to means. When the 'tug of war' between health and social care budgets is minimised, and the two providers work collaboratively, then outcomes for patients and staff can be much improved, and likely savings made. 'We're not great, as a sector, at working together, there could be significant improvements to health and social care if we were joined up, it's sad we're not' (care home group owner).

This issue was considered in Chapter 2, in respect of the Neighbourhood Cares and Wellbeing Teams models, where medical needs, nursing and social care were brought together under one community delivery umbrella. There are other examples of this type of collaboration, such as the Vanguard Programmes being rolled out across England and Wales (commentary to be found in https://www.enhertsvanguard.uk/media/format/journal-article).

These put 'clear plans in place for managing demand more effectively across the local health system and ... reduce costs, whilst at the same time improving the care provided to patients. These savings include reducing avoidable hospital admissions and bed days, releasing back office savings and improving prevention, self-care and the use of technology' (Jones, 2016, no page number). In one instance of a care home in Hertfordshire:

> A local GP has been linked to the home and a pharmacist is working with residents to ensure they only take the medication they need. In March there were no falls – before the scheme there were about eight a month. Ambulance calls are down more than 30 per cent.

The Community Health Support Team Model described in *My Home Life* (Help the Aged, 2007, p. 103) 'comprises older people's specialist nurses (OPSNs), a mental health lead nurse, pharmacist, part-time old age psychiatrist, two consultant geriatrician sessions per week, and three sessions per week from one consultant nurse.' This has enabled cross-specialist training and an interface between primary care and care homes. The outcomes of moving away from silo working are not only cost-savings and improved job satisfaction as noted but, most importantly, older people benefit from continuity of care and carers. However, these models of good practice are developed and sustained locally, and as one interviewee said, lack of continuity of care is a problem for which 'there is no countrywide approach. Nothing that's going to solve it systemically, there's a wider inherent issue which is to be addressed at the top'. Practitioners can learn from good models, but it is essential that policy makers do likewise.

Transfer from living in the family home to a residential setting brings more issues and heartache and illustrates the over-complexity of the system: Adult Social Care support may be available from an LA, while Funded Nursing Care (FNC) paid for by the NHS may be available for community-based nursing care – although not adequate to cover all needs – but then impossible to transfer to residential care, in effect closing the doors to many facilities. Continued Healthcare Funding may then cut in – or may not – depending on a lengthy needs assessment, during which health status has probably changed and become more expensive to manage.

These issues come with a high human cost; as the daughter of an ageing and ill lady trapped in this system said: 'It shocked me how poor the system is and how un-joined up it is. People don't speak to families at all. For people who don't know how the sector works, they don't stand a hope. No hope whatsoever.'

Public and private (for-profit and not-for-profit) delivery of care also leads to significant variation and injustices. At its worst, such variation can be seen in the healthcare setting between NHS and private wards, as described by Watson during her work as a nurse: 'Along the corridor is the private patients' ward….It is another world. They seem to have everything and never run out' (2018, p. 289).

In the social care context, it is not so simplistic as 'expensive is best', but rather that a system which accommodates more than one basis for delivery leads to different priorities and expectations that are often very dependent on the philosophies of owners or managers. As Culliford says:

> It is easier to remain truthful, and set a fair price, if what you offer is useful, of good quality…it is easier to serve others, and profit the community

as well as oneself, if you take the trouble to listen patiently, find out what people really need.

(2020, p. 76)

The argument for relational care must be made for each model from large corporation to independent enterprise, but the factors which favour it may be easier to install in one rather than another.

Certainly smaller private providers, if they are of sufficient size to have good systems and management, can be more flexible than the large publicly quoted corporates and can choose to focus more on residents' wellbeing, as the financial director of one such explained when I interviewed him: 'We have the flexibility to make decisions which enhance resident experience; for instance we don't have to wait ten years to refurbish a care home but can go on a needs basis rather than a rigid system. If we had a different financial arrangement and structure maybe that wouldn't be as easy. Once that decision is made it happens very quickly whereas another [big corporate] organisation may take years because of financial restraint.' The regional manager of another small group said:

> It's a private company and we're lucky, our directors are happy if we're talking about improving the lives of our residents, morale of staff, they'll make the investment. We've been owned by the same two families for 35 years. When I talk to managers in bigger groups (for instance at meetings) they spend their time talking to councils and NHS about fees.

Seven of the 18 largest privately owned care homes, for example, 'spend between 15 and 32 per cent of their revenue on rent payments...This stands in marked contrast to the eight largest not-for-profit providers, which spend an aggregate of 2 per cent of their income on rent' (report in **i** newspaper, 9.11.19). These figures are taken from a Centre for Health and Public Interest (CHPI) report that warned of 'hundreds of millions of pounds [from the care sector] going to offshore investors'. Writing during the Covid-19 pandemic, Ian Birrell notes the millions of pounds being paid in dividends to the founders and directors of large, publicly quoted care providers, the 'big private players' who took over social care in the wake of austerity when the NHS was spared the worst. He summarises that 'staff on the frontline are paid peanuts while their bosses pocket fortunes' ('We need to care for the carers', **i** newspaper, 6.4.20).

The wellbeing of the industry, and those who work in it or rely on it, may be upheld by some highly ethical private operators, but clearly there is no external guarantee of this, and CHPI calls for 'the UK care home industry to be restructured so more money goes to frontline services and for the Government to use more money to build new care homes'.

Such a call to build would only result in overall benefits if publicly funded homes did not become a Cinderella service. There is no logical reason they should, given the excellence of some not-for-profit operators, who are standard bearers for the best in relational care, but there is a danger that they would.

Aiming to attract those most able to pay, who may be the relatives rather than the resident, can result in an emphasis on appearance and the type of facilities that would grace a hotel rather than a real home. Gawande describes visiting friends in a retirement community in the United States:

> It was like a nice hotel, only with no-one under seventy-five walking around.... Even in an average community, rent runs $32,000 (£25,300) a year. Entry fees are $60,000 to $120,000 (£47,600 to £95,240) on top of that... the median income of people aged eighty and over if $15,000 (£11,900).

The gap between what is likely to be affordable and the cost of hotel-style living is stark.

Clearly, creating buildings and facilities demands very substantial investment – into the tens of millions. When there are shareholders requiring a return on investment, or there is a high debt ratio or scaling up is too speedy, then rent and services must be priced at a premium. If the investor or owner is a publicly quoted company, as opposed to a private limited company or not-for-profit, it will have little room for manoeuvre to plough any excess back into developments that are not immediately perceived to attract more 'customers' – in other words, the longer-term and more subtle developments and staff costs that promote relational care – and certainly not to help subsidise the less affluent. The smaller private company can control scaling speed and debt ratio more easily and may even be able to cross-subsidise excellent care if it diversifies into other business areas but will still be constrained on what it can offer by each LA's weekly allocation for care payment. This means that there is a marked geographical inequality partly due to variation in land values of different areas in the country, and partly due to variations in LA allocations.

Big businesses providing support services for older people, whether these are domiciliary care or housing, do not have a good track record of survival. One thinks of Carillion and Southern Cross, which had to cease trading suddenly and went into liquidation in 2018 and 2011 respectively, and the fracture and loss of relationships as well as employment that resulted.

Yet government remains more comfortable dealing with big business and 'most of its subsidies and corporate welfare programmes go to the largest companies' (Horesh, 2008, p. 40). While smaller private sector bodies have to be disciplined as well as market-responsive to survive, public sector bodies and large corporations contracting to them 'distort...the market' (ibid., p. 45) and are no longer directly accountable to those they serve (other than through the ballot box).

Gawande describes how the drive towards bigger businesses can pervert a humane concept, telling the story of assisted living in the United States. Founder Keren Wilson's original idea was profitable, but her board and Wall Street demanded 'even bigger profits'. Wilson 'wanted to build smaller buildings in smaller towns... for low income elderly... but the more profitable direction was bigger buildings in bigger towns without low-income clientele' (2014, p. 102). Eventually she sold all her shares, and her original, inspired idea developed into a worldwide industry in which standards have declined such that by 2003 only 11% of assisted living facilities in the United States were able to offer the services on which they were originally predicated. A survey of the pioneering assisted living facilities 15 years earlier had shown that tenants thrived and 'the cost for those on government support was 20 percent lower than it would have been in a nursing home' (ibid., p. 91). The concept morphed from saving the public purse, to creating private wealth at public cost.

Smaller operators, those that act in smaller semi-autonomous units and those with enlightened and flexible management – whether charitable or businesses, are in a better position to appreciate how change and innovation affect the well-being of older people and carers who are involved in their enterprise. They need just as much financial acumen as any other business but can prioritise keeping the business stable, and thus reduce the risk to residents and staff of forced closure. 'Keeping the residents at the core of decision making is really essential. We always say good care equals good business which puts us in a good position', as one financial director explained to me. Certainly, lower staff turnover can save a lot of money, given that Skills for Care calculate a cost of around £8,000 for the recruitment and induction of one person. Good reputation also saves money: 'We don't have to advertise to fill our beds; it's word of mouth' (owner of an independent home).

In this respect, being able to track the actual cost savings of good relational care would be a great advantage. Such savings are indicated, although more research in the UK would be very welcome. Gawande gives a detailed account of the translation of Chase Memorial Nursing Home in the United States, transformed from an 'institution' into a 'real home' with staff responsibilities redesigned for interaction and the introduction of pets, gardens and on-site childcare amongst other changes.

> Researchers studied the effects of this program over two years, comparing a variety of measures for Chase's residents with those of residents at another nursing home nearby. Their study found that the number of prescriptions required per resident fell to half that of the control nursing home. Psychotropic drugs for agitation ... decreased in particular. The total drug costs fell to just 38 percent of the comparison facility. Deaths fell 15 percent.
>
> (Gawande, 2014, p. 123)

Not surprisingly, this book would argue strongly for recognition not only of savings to individuals or the public purse but also for the intrinsic social value of the wellbeing of elders and all who care for them; we are more than 'humans as economic ciphers whose value can be defined [only] in economic terms' (Koch, 2000, p. 7). However, as Barnes et al. warn, this does not mean money is irrelevant: 'Wellbeing may not be determined by increased personal wealth but failing to act against rising inequality will not enhance wellbeing' (2018, p. 127).

Who makes the choices for older people?

Common sense suggests that older people, and those helping and advising them, would be more likely to choose the sort of programmes and facilities that are based on fostering good relationships, rather than those that favour appearance over substance and do not offer the same benefits. However, choices are influenced by whether it is possible to gather information in time and 'test drive' the options – and as we saw when considering issues relating to transition, decision making may not have the luxury of time. There are other factors of course: availability, capacity to use facilities that are available, cost, personal inclination amongst others.

Further, decisions can be skewed by perceptions promoted by the market: one's own and those of people advising and influencing. Consumer research, as opposed to listening attentively and with an open mind to the voices of older people, is predicated on a consumer-style 'market': 'the consumerist rhetoric of 'voice and choice' effectively becomes the smokescreen for the further dismantling of collective responsibilities and increased individualism' (Barnes et al., 2018, p. 67).

Similarly, whether care is self or public funded will affect choices. There is an argument that self-funding may result in individuals appointing and directing their own carers and hence 'help to foster more personal interaction and caring relationships' (Cluff and Binstock, 2001, p. 171), but as few older people are likely to have the business and employment knowledge to manage this sort of supply and regulation, it is more likely that self-funders will purchase care through a 'constrain[ing] bureaucratic agency' (ibid.). Otherwise they will face finding and managing care services themselves without sufficient advice and face the 'risks of their care needs not being adequately met, the risk of poor purchasing decisions with adverse financial implications and the risk of exploitation or abuse from agencies whose prime concern may be profit and survival' (Barnes et al., 2018, p. 179).

In some cases, advice and help may be forthcoming from friends or, more likely, relatives. Family support remains an underlying assumption in the care system with 'policies that firmly state that people should and want to remain in their own homes and with their families. These policies increasingly rely on family support' (Mowat and Mowat, 2018, p. 105). Not only may this be unavailable, but even when it is, family may not have the knowledge or information to make judgements about what is the 'best' for their loved one, either being overly careful and restricting them or urging them to activity and 'doing' rather than 'being'. Gawande summarises this phenomenon as: 'We want autonomy for ourselves, and safety for those we love' (2014, p. 106).

In the end, choices are often forced on older people and their families by urgency to act and policy that dictates what is available, how it is resourced and the processes to access support; sadly, this can lead not only to a reduction in autonomy but in safety as well.

Challenging policy

Current policy in the UK presents two major challenges to good, relational care that must be addressed: silo working – particularly but not only the dislocation between health and personal care in terms of funding, provision and accountability – and assumptions about the value of people (of older citizens and of the caring workforce) and their place in society. Both challenges arise from established theories shared across the political divide about the need for older people to give way to the younger generation and disengage from work, yet also to age 'successfully' by staying as healthy and active as possible and minimising their calls on the public purse.

Theories can quickly become prescriptive, and then become the norm, then 'politically laden' (Mowat and Mowat, 2018, p. 53) and then finally embedded.

> Governments ... are happy to pursue failed policies as long as these policies have been done before. Supporting a failed but conventional policy is less risky ... than supporting a new one, even one that is far more likely to succeed.
>
> *(Horesh, 2008, p. 157)*

Low expectations of older people are a self-fulfilling prophecy if they lead to 'lack of opportunity' and other 'artificial and external constraints' (Woodward, 2008, p. 21), while high expectations of independence see the ageing condemned to feeling themselves a failure. One might say, indeed, that they are damned if they do and damned if they don't!

The history of key themes in social policy in the UK over the period 2000 to 2007 is traced by Woodward (ibid., pp. 181 to 186) as an upward trajectory towards greater choice and more joined-up thinking; however, he also notes the enduring challenge 'to leave behind the legacy of the Poor Law' and its 're-minders of the workhouse', which mean that current policies 'are still focussed on determining who is *not* entitled to assistance' (ibid., p. 187). Unfortunately, this hopeful direction of progress in the early 2000s seems to have remained unfulfilled, perhaps impeded by austerity measures, ministerial changes and the Brexit focus. In 2020 the engrained assumptions about ageing, the resulting age-ism and destructive divisions within the funding system still need to be tackled if resource is to be directed towards improved wellbeing across the spectrum of older adult care.

Why does relational care matter?

Part of the answer must be to reconsider the ethics of sharing resources, the more so when they are perceived to be more limited than previously, due to the rhetoric of austerity and the challenges of climate change. In this context, it is worth remembering the Health Foundation poll cited above: people may well be willing to pay more for social care via general taxation if it is seen to be a fair system with better outcomes.

Given longevity predictions, many of us will reach a time in life where we will be affected by a policy that is currently ageist in its 'allocation of public resources in ways that assume a lesser priority for the needs of old people in comparison to younger people' (Barnes et al., 2018, p. 141). Nor should we forget that denying resource to older people affects the whole of society by depressing the working conditions and pay of carers, demoting their value by assuming they are 'unskilled', placing greater burdens on the NHS and affecting the economy through lost input due to unpaid care provided by friends and family.

Yet this situation can be improved if influencers and policy makers listen to the voices of older people and their carers and start to shift resource towards positively funding and encouraging the factors that underpin good relational care, whereby all involved can thrive and as a result can save the higher costs of 'picking up the pieces' when older people fail to get the community interventions or residential care they require at the optimum time or in the most appropriate way.

'The collective counter stories of those living ageing [must be] recognised by decision-makers and used to inform policy' (Barnes et al., 2018, p. 15), and until that time, there will be a gap between the actual experience of growing older and the 'discourses that frame ageing within policy' (ibid.). Following the closure of the UK Advisory Forum on Ageing in 2015, there has been no official channel for older peoples' voices to be heard by government, although there is of course a flow of information and campaigning from the third sector.

Older peoples' lives can be transformed by the right support; and nothing less than a transformation in policy to underpin better practice and happier outcomes is urgently needed.

The alternative to radical change in the UK is a drift towards the US model, so tellingly described and decried by Dodson and Zincavage in Chapter 1, where an extreme neoliberal ideology dictates that older people in need of care should be provided for by their own assets until these are exhausted; should then live with families, willing or unwilling; and finally if both these options are depleted may get very limited help from a state source such as Medicaid. With each move through the system, there is debilitating anxiety and fractured relationships. In contrast, the concept of 'care ethics' offers a positive way of approaching policy to enable deeper dialogue about old age and a complete reconsideration of its assumptions. The practice of relational care described in this book indicates where that dialogue might lead in terms of practice and planning.

In all the complexity of funding sources and continual fluctuation of policy, and the knowledge of what could be achieved in the future if these were to be simplified and focussed on the concept of flourishing for all involved in care, it is all too easy to lose sight of what matters and what can be achieved right now. Once the premise of the benefits of relational care is accepted, we already have the tools to make it happen.

Some further reading relating to this chapter

Availability and funding of care

Older People's Care Survey, Cottell, J, 2017, Family and Childcare Trust.

Balancing good care and financial issues

The Compassionate and Commercially Aware Care Manager, Hawkins, R, 2017, Hawker Publications.

Enabling older people to make their own decisions

Knowledge Exchange with Older People through an Ethic of Care (KEOPEC): This project grounds research in a central framework of care ethics, resulting in a suite of learning resources such as films and booklets to help practitioners involve older people in decisions about care. The resources can be accessed at: https://www.brighton.ac.uk/research-and-enterprise/groups/social-science-policy/research-projects/older-people-wellbeing-and-participation.aspx

Policy and care ethics

Engster, D. and Hamington, M. (2015) *Care Ethics and Political Theory*, Oxford: Oxford University Press.

Ageism

A recent report by the Centre for Ageing Better provides a literature review and commentary: *Doddery but Dear? Examining Age-Related Stereotypes* (2020), accessible on https://www.ageing-better.org.uk/publications/doddery-dear-examining-age-related-stereotypes

APPENDIX A

MEASURING AND EVALUATING WELLBEING

Introduction

Throughout this book, reference has been made to measuring the effectiveness of different models of care. If there is no element of assessment, proponents of a particular model may be working on a well-founded 'hunch', a feeling that they have got something right. There is much to be said for that, if it is backed up by extensive interaction and recording with the people most affected. How do they feel about their situation, and what do they believe most influences those feelings? However, this may not be sufficient to convince policy makers. Nor will it necessarily convince the public and private-sector bodies paying for services: they will need evidence or strong indicators that their funds are being invested in the optimum way and, preferably, that improvements in how people feel about their lives are being translated into savings, such as reduced medication.

Establishing any type of accepted measurement system is difficult, as it demands targets that are realistic, agreed between parties, consistently measurable, yet sufficiently flexible to take account of changes in external circumstances. Additionally, targets can influence delivery focus, and not necessarily for the better (an issue in the NHS, for example). This book does not attempt to offer expertise in the matter, but it does attempt to raise awareness that measurement is an underlying consideration and to provide some ideas about what is already available in the field of wellbeing and where to find resources.

Insofar as care of older people is concerned, the independent regulator of all health and social care (including care at home, community services and care homes) in England is the Care Quality Commission (CQC). This is a public body, which sets and monitors fundamental standards, inspects and rates schemes and has enforcement powers to demand improvements and hold providers accountable through suspension, cancelled registration and even criminal proceedings. Its equivalents in the devolved nations are Care Inspectorates in Scotland and Wales, and the Regulation and Quality Improvement Authority in Northern Ireland.

Deciding what to measure

One of the key questions when considering the usefulness and validity of a method is its purpose. On the one hand, for the provider of care, this may be, for example, to meet external requirements such as regulatory or shareholder reporting; as a basis for future planning and investment; and to gather marketing or training material. They will wish to know how the project or home is functioning overall, and welfare of clients is only one factor in the assessment. On the other hand, older people and their families will be primarily interested in levels of wellbeing of the clients, especially before making any decisions about providers. Additionally, staff will need feedback on how they and their employers are doing.

Fulfilling these varied purposes goes beyond hard data; moreover, the focus on obtaining and using limited 'hard data' can result in 'statistical reductionism', against which Cluff and Binstock warn: 'crucial soft data and complex phenomena are overlooked, and the resulting reports are about 'average' rather than real people' (2001, p. 212). The danger is that real people become the subjects of an overall judgement but have not actually been listened to. 'Developing policies and practices …requires a more grounded and contextualised way of approaching how people make sense of what is happening in their lives and what it is they value' (Barnes et al., 2018, p. 130).

This important distinction between the provider and the client perspective is made by Reed in *My Home Life*:

> Quality of life is often confused with quality of care, which is the way in which care is delivered and the standards that it meets. Separating quality of life from quality of care is a difficult process, especially as the two are interconnected. If care is of a high standard, it can support and promote quality of life. Nevertheless, quality of life can be independent of quality of care.
>
> *(2007, Help the Aged, p. 24)*

She goes on to say that there is a need to

> mov[e] away from a needs-based view to a preferences perspective. … This may involve relinquishing professional models of quality of life based on needs as defined by professionals. …Thinking about preferences means having a much more 'older person-based' perspective on quality of life … talking with them about their views.
>
> *(Ibid., p. 26)*

Tools developed for assessing care of older people

Only once an organisation has decided what it wants to measure, and why, can it choose the best tool. There are many available, some of the following have been referred to in this book. Considering the pressing need to have better ways of evaluating and championing relational care, it would be excellent if one or more could form the basis of a method that could be developed and piloted: a challenge that is beyond the scope of this book.

Your Care Rating

The largest survey of care home residents in the UK, this evaluation has been developed and is conducted annually by Ipsos MORI. It is particularly useful in the context of relational care, as it prioritises the voices of residents, using an extensively tested paper questionnaire with which family and friends can assist. The perceptions of relatives are also factored in. The objective is to get feedback on: feelings about life and services in the home, care and support, staff and managers, satisfaction with care, likelihood of recommending the care home and personal background information. For the 2018/2019 survey, 19 care home providers participated, and a total of 11,188 residents took part across 532 homes, resulting in a searchable database particularly useful to older people and their families choosing a care home.

Thomas Tool

This has been developed by Kirsty Thomas and the Hallmark Care Home group, as part of its commitment to relationship-centred care. It is designed to measure risk of social isolation, using a decision-tree model based on key factors in social isolation identified through research carried out internally and by Age UK. As it is directed towards use in dementia care, the evaluation of a resident is undertaken by the team members closest to the person. It results not only in a risk assessment but also in a profile and plan of action that takes into account an individual's preferences; not just what they enjoy but also their natural mode of engagement, whether it be gregarious or more solitary. For example, one person's needs may be very well met without them taking part in group activities. Once a plan is drawn up, its success can be monitored by observing the resident and what engages them, which may be active participation or just enjoying watching others. Insofar as social isolation is concerned, the underlying risk level may not change, but its expression in actual isolation can be addressed and significantly altered to improve contentment and purpose in life.

The Purpose in Life (PIL) test

This is a psychometric instrument designed by Crumbaugh and Maholik to measure meaning in life. It comprises a questionnaire and individual therapy sections and is widely used. 'The test is standardised and validated....More than 50 PhD dissertations have been written which employ the PIL test as a major measuring tool' (Jewell, 2004, p. 119).

ICECAP

'Capability wellbeing' encompasses a variety of health and non-health dimensions that may be difficult to separate. ICECAP stands for 'Investigating Choice Experiments in Capability' and is used as ICECAP-A for the general population and ICECAP-O for those over 65. It has been developed to capture all the benefits (physical, psychological and social) of health and care models when they are subject to economic assessments.

Frameworks and profiling

Various 'frameworks' have also been developed for organising and benchmarking the nature of care delivered to older people. These are not strictly measurement systems but are used by some care homes (including a number referenced in this book) to provide benchmarks against which different elements of care can be judged. Some are used by care homes as a mark of quality, indicating standards and attitudes which clients can expect.

The Butterfly Model

The Butterfly Model, developed by Dr David Sheard of Dementia Care Matters, is based on prioritising feelings over dictating behaviours, enabling staff to be more flexible in terms of allocating their time and being alongside those with dementia. Outcomes such as including more relaxed routines and changes to the physical environment can be tracked, but additionally it is possible to measure changes in the incidence of specific occurrences. In terms of impact, Wren Hall collated hard data as well as qualitative evidence and found that following the adoption of the Butterfly Model (which is very similar to the model that promotes good relational care), there was: '43% reduced incidence of falls, 58% reduced incidence of expressed 'behaviours' and 35% reduction in the staff sickness figure' (Sheard, 2013, Dementia Care Matters, no page numbers).

The Eden Alternative

The Eden Alternative is a worldwide movement initiated in the United States, based on the core belief that ageing should be a continued stage of development and growth, rather than a period of decline. It proposes creating a 'human habitat', a home where residents can participate in caring for themselves, other people and their surroundings in an enhanced environment where staff and residents are empowered to make decisions. The philosophy is about helping care homes to move away from task orientation and towards supporting a meaningful life for all those they care for and combatting the plagues of loneliness, helplessness and boredom that make life intolerable in so many homes. Although it is not part of any regulatory system or other quality mark, it holds a register of UK care homes that have joined its course, have committed to and are implementing the Eden philosophy.

Relational Proximity Framework

The Relationships Foundation is a think tank that explores different ways in which public policy, organisations and individual behaviour shape the relationships that influence the wellbeing of individuals and communities. The Foundation develops relational audit tools for health and social care designed to address how the relational experience of giving and receiving care can be protected within highly pressured systems and how the role of relationships, as both an aspect and a determinant of health, can be given greater prominence in policy and practice. Its measurement tools include the Relational Proximity Framework, based on questionnaires that indicate the distance in a relationship between two people or organisations. This enables a determination of how well each engages with the thinking, emotions and behaviour of the other, resulting in a framework map.

The Senses Framework and CARE profiles

This Framework was developed primarily for the nursing profession, where relationships are likely to be more transient, and although it encourages 'enriched' environments of care in which the needs of all groups are accorded equal value, status and significance' (Nolan et al., 2006, p. 10), its original driver concerning retention of nurses means that it does focus more on student gerontological nurses than on other groups. It used workshops including older people and their families to define and refine the 'six senses' identified as key to the creation of good care environments and as such might inform the development of qualitative measuring tools for elderly social care: 'the Senses were acknowledged as providing a way of realising a "vision" of care in which the "fundamental" components were valued and accorded status' (ibid., p. 106).

The Combined Assessment of Residential Environments (CARE) profiling tool was developed on the basis of the Senses Framework. Early experiences of using CARE in different care homes suggested that this approach could provide a way of recognising good practice and outcomes as well as supporting change (Faulkner and Davies., 2006) but does not appear to have been developed yet.

Resources and further reading

Care Inspectorate Scotland www.healthcareimprovementscotland.org
Care Inspectorate Wales https://careinspectorate.wales

Care Quality Commission https://www.cqc.org.uk/

'ICECAP-O, the current state of play: a systematic review of studies reporting the psychometric properties and use of the instrument over the decade since its publication', Proud, McLoughlin and Kinghorn in *Quality of Life Research* (2019) 28, pp. 1429–1439.

In *My Home Life*, Help the Aged, 2007, Section 3 'Quality of Care' by Davis and Heath reviews a number of tools applicable to care homes.

In *The Lost Art of Caring*, Cluff and Binstock, Chapter 10 'Appraising the Success of Caring' by Feinstein gives an overview of some of the issues with measurement.

Mattering in a dementia care home – The Butterfly Approach, Sheard, 2012, Dementia Care Matters https://www.dementiacarematters.com/pdf/modern.pdf

Poster summary of the Senses Framework https://www.sheffield.ac.uk/polopoly_fs/1.811379!/file/Senses_Framework_Posters.pdf

Regulation and Quality Improvement Authority https://www.rqia.org.uk/

'The CARE (Combined Assessment of Residential Environments) profiles: a new approach to improving quality in care homes', Faulkner, M. and Davies, S. (2006), *Quality in Ageing and Older Adults*, Vol. 7, No. 3, pp. 15–25.

The Eden Alternative www.eden-alternative.co.uk

The Relationships Foundation https://relationshipsfoundation.org/

The Senses Framework: improving care for older people through a relationship-centred approach. Getting Research into Practice (GRiP) Report No 2. Project Report, Nolan, Brown, Davies, Nolan and Keady, 2006, University of Sheffield http://shura.shu.ac.uk/280/1/PDF_Senses_Framwork_Report.pdf

Your Care Rating https://www.yourcarerating.org/

APPENDIX B

NOTES ON SURVEYS AND SCOPE OF THE BOOK

Listening to older people and their carers

The Abbeyfield Society survey referred to in this book is described in full in Woodward and Kartupelis (2018) pp. 43 to 45. It took place between 2014 and 2016 and included 100 one-to-one semi-structured interviews in 40 different care homes. Most importantly, these interviews were not only with residents but also with managers, care staff and volunteers.

The findings of the survey were notable, in that there was a high level of consensus about what really mattered to people and helped them to thrive. There was also a striking similarity in the ways they described how they felt about what mattered: mutual support and love, trust and security, a sense of meaning and purpose, a feeling of belonging to a home and family and a sense of being valued. These feelings represent the key criteria for relational care, and equally it was possible to define the environmental factors that support their delivery.

I believe it was only possible to form this understanding by listening to the voices of people for whom these matters were the warp and weft of their daily lives, which I was privileged to share briefly. It felt like an obligation to play some part in ensuring the voices were heard. However, the Abbeyfield study was limited in that it took place only in care homes, and in only one (although diverse) organisation. Would the findings apply to other care delivery models such as community-based teams, other organisations and other approaches? What other good practice was happening in the UK? This book is based on 50 more interviews, using the same semi-structured method, but in a much wider variety of settings. In this case, the survey was not commissioned by any organisation but facilitated by many organisations who were generous with their time and interest in the work. All interviews were given with informed consent (both in the original and subsequent surveys) and are anonymised. Organisations have been named in such a way that it would not be possible to identify individuals within them.

The intention was to be able to offer ideas, information and learning to a wide audience, including older people and their families; owners and managers of public-, private- and third-sector organisations delivering care; employed and voluntary carers; and students with an interest in the issues. Therefore, the models chosen and described in this book are intended to be examples of best and innovative practice, not selected as a random, broadly representative sample of the industry but as a source of inspiration that could be distilled into information of practical use.

In several respects, the information in this book will, I trust, fulfil a need by using the approach of being 'alongside' the interviewees, focussing on processes rather than outcomes, which, as Mowat and Mowat say, 'has been surprisingly absent from training programmes in health and social care' (2018, p. 82). It reflects the lived experience of a large number of diverse people, shared in the setting of their own environment, which could, therefore, be used as an additional, contextual source. Relying on a single interviewer rather than a team has pros and cons: the findings will be 'mediated ... narratives in which I was an active audience, whose reaction necessarily influenced the flow of the story itself' (Koch, 2000, p. 13) but equally the interviewees become 'co-researchers' rather than research subjects. They are enabled to lead parts of the conversation, introduce new ideas and direct the focus to what they feel matters most.

Scope

Dementia issues

The relevance of the observations in this book to older people with dementia has already been raised: while some approaches do need to be adapted, the philosophy and practice of relational care, its foundations, key criteria and environmental factors all hold good. Therefore, there are few specific references to dementia as a separate issue. However, there is a very wide literature on the subject, for families, practitioners and academic study, far too wide to reference below (e.g., a simple search on Amazon yields over 3,000 tittles). The information in the resources below is provided because it has particular relevance to relational care.

Families as carers

Similarly, this book only refers to families in the context of professional care provision. Care of older people by their families and other unpaid carers was estimated by the Office of National Statistics (ONS) to be £56.9 billion in the UK in 2014, and in 2015/2016, 8% of the UK's private household population were "informal carers" for someone (information from ONS web site dated 10 July 2017, accessed 26 March 2020). This is a very substantial contribution to care, and not surprisingly, there is again a large number of publications addressing a diverse audience on all aspects of the subject. In the context of relational care, it cannot be assumed that relatives will provide the best; they may offer the perfect family setting of love, understanding and acceptance; they may be harsh, greedy and vindictive; or they may be normal humans who can be kind, loving, angry, tired and conflicted.

Further reading

Dementia

Chapter Six 'Dementia Homes' in Woodward and Kartupelis, 2018, pp. 95–118.
Chapter Ten 'Magic Mirrors' by John Killick in Jewell ed., 2004, pp. 143–152.
The Wilderness by Samantha Harvey (2009) is a perceptive novel that explores the journey into Alzheimer's and helps in understanding dementia from the inside and outside perspectives.

BIBLIOGRAPHY

Adult Social Care Funding, State of the Nation Report (2016) London: Local Government Association.

Albans, K. and Johnson, M. (eds.) (2013) *God, Me and Being Very Old*, London: SCM Press.

As Time Goes By (2013) https://www.brighton.ac.uk/ssparc/researc-projects/older-people-wellbeing-and-participation.aspx

Baker, C. (2013) 'Measuring the F factor – Happiness, resilience and spiritual capital in public policy', paper given at the *Spirituality and Addiction Conference*: 20 February 2013, University of Chester, Chester Centre for Faiths and Public Policy.

Barken, R. and Lowndes, R. (2018) 'Supporting family involvement in long-term residential care: Promising practices for relational care', *Qualitative Health Research*. DOI: 10.1177%2F1049732317730568

Barnes, M. (2012) *Care in Everyday Life, an Ethic of Care in Practice*, Bristol: Policy Press.

Barnes, M. (2019) 'Community care: The ethics of care in a residential community,' *Ethics and Social Welfare* DOI: 10.1080/17496535.2019.1652334

Barnes, M., Gahagan, B. and Ward, L. (2018) *Re-imaging Old Age: Wellbeing, Care and Participation*, Wilmington: Vernon Press.

Booth, R. Lack of homes suitable for older people fuels housing crisis – report, *The Guardian*, 14 July 2019.

Brooker, D. (2004) 'What is Person Centred Care for people with dementia?' *Reviews in Clinical Gerontology*, 13(3), 215–222.

Chittister, J.D. (2008) *The Gift of Years*, London: Darton Longman & Todd.

Cluff, M.D. and Binstock, R.H. (eds.) (2001) *The Lost Art of Caring*, Baltimore: Johns Hopkins University Press.

Cottell, J. (2017) *Older People's Care Survey*, London: Family and Childcare Trust.

Crisp, R. (2015) *The Social Brain: How Diversity Made the Modern Mind*, London: Robinson.

Cromby, J. (2011) 'The greatest gift? Happiness, governance and psychology' *Social and Personality Psychology Compass*, 5(11), 840–852.

Culliford, L. (2015) *Much Ado about Something*, London: SPCK.

Culliford, L. (2020) *The Big Book of Wisdom*, London: Hero.

Dahlberg, L. and McKee, K.J. (2014) 'Correlates of Social and Emotional Loneliness in Older People: Evidence From an English Community Study' *Aging Mental Health*, doi: 10.1080/13607863.2013.856863. Epub 2013 Nov 19.

Davidson, S. and Rossall, P. (2015) *Evidence Review: Loneliness in Later Life*, London: AgeUK.

Department for Work and Pensions (2017) Family Resources Survey: financial year 2015/16. [Online] Available at: https://www.gov.uk/government/statistics/family-resources-surveyfinancial-year-201516

Dimnet, E. (1932) *What We Live By*, London: Simon & Schuster.

Doddery But Dear? Examining Age-related Stereotypes (2020) https://www.ageing-better.org.uk/publications/doddery-dear-examining-age-related-stereotypes

Dodson, L. and Zincavage, R. (2007) '"It's like a family": Caring labor, exploitation, and race in nursing homes', *Gender and Society*, 21(6), 905–928, Sage Publications.

Drennan V.M., Ross F., Saunders, M. and West, P. (2017) *The Guy's and St Thomas' NHS Foundation Trust Neighbourhood Nursing Team Test and Learn Project of an Adapted Buurtzorg Model: An Early View*, London: Centre for Health & Social Care Research.

Duerden, N. (2018) *Life Less Lonely, a: What We Can All Do to Lead More Connected, Kinder Lives*, London: Bloomsbury.

Engster, D. and Hamington, M. (2015) *Care Ethics and Political Theory*, Oxford: Oxford University Press.

Faulkner, M. and Davies, S. (2006), 'The CARE (Combined Assessment of Residential Environments) profiles: a new approach to improving quality in care homes', *Quality in Ageing and Older Adults*, 7(3), 15–25.

Gallagher, A. (2017) 'Care ethics and nursing practice,' (Chapter 15) in *Key Concepts and Issues in Nursing Ethics*, edited by P.A. Scott, New York Springer.

Gallagher, A. (2020) *Slow Ethics and the Art of Care*, Bingley: Emerald Publishing.

Gallagher, A. and Herbert, C. (eds.) (2019) *Faith and Ethics in Health and Social Care: Improving Practice through Understanding Diverse Perspectives*, London: Jessica Kingsley Publishers.

Gawande, A. (2014) *Being Mortal, Illness, Medicine and What Matters in the End*, London: Profile Books.

Hand, C., et al., (2020) 'Enacting agency – Exploring how older adults shape their neighbourhoods', *Ageing and Society*, 40(3), 565–583.

Hare Duke, M. (2001) *One Foot in Heaven: Growing Older and Living to the Full*, London: Triangle/SPCK.

Harvey, S. (2009) *The Wilderness*, New York: Nan A. Talese.

Hawkins, R. (2017) *The Compassionate and Commercially Aware Care Manager,* London: Hawker Publications.

Healthwatch England (2015) *Safely Home: What Happens When Older People Leave Hospital and Care Settings*, London: Healthwatch England Special Enquiry Findings.

Help the Aged (2007) *My Home Life: Quality of Life in Care Homes*, London: National Care Homes Research and Development Forum.

Hertzberg, A. and Ekman, S. (2003) "We, not them and us?' Views on the relationships and interactions between staff and relatives of older people permanently living in nursing homes,' *Journal of Advanced Nursing*, 31(3), 614–622.

Holstein, M. (2015) *Women in Later Life: Critical Perspectives on Gender and Age*, Lanham: Rowan & Littlefield.

Horesh, R. (2008) *Market Solutions for Social and Environmental Problems: Social Policy Bonds*, www.SocialGoals.com

Hugo, L. (2005) *Where the Trail Grows Faint: A Year in the Life of a Dog Therapy Team*, Lincoln and London: University of Nebraska Press.

Hupkens, S. et al. (2016) 'Meaning in life of older persons: An integrative literature review', *Nursing Ethics*, 21.12.2016, doi: 10.1177%2F0969733016680122

Innovation and Technology in Care Homes (2016) The SEHTA Review, https://www.se-hta.co.uk/cms-data/depot/sehta/Technology-Innovation-in-Care-Homes-The-SEHTA-Review.pdf

Jewell, A. (ed.) (2004) *Ageing, Spirituality and Well-being*, London, Jessica Kingsley Publishers.

Jones, S. (2016) *Vanguard Programmes*, https://www.enhertsvanguard.uk/media/format/journal-article

Karner, T.X. (1998) 'Professional caring: Home care worker as fictive kin', *Journal of Aging Studies* 12(1), 69–82.

Kartupelis, J. (2015) 'Spiritual life in homes shared by older people', *Working with Older People*, 19(3)/Emerald (14.7.2015), 150.

Kartupelis, J. (2016) 'Exploring the dynamics of spiritual life in residential care communities', *Journal for the Study of Spirituality* (January 2016), doi: 10.1179/2044024315Z.00000000049.

Killick, J. (2013) *Dementia Positive: A Handbook Based on Lived Experiences*, Edinburgh: Luath Press.

Killick, J. and Allan, K. (2001) *Communication and the Care of People with Dementia*, Maidenhead: Open University Press.

King, U. (2004) 'The Dance of Life: Spirituality, ageing and human flourishing,' (Chapter 9) in *Ageing, Spirituality an Wellbeing*, edited by A. Jewell, London: Jessica Kingsley Publishers.

Koch, T. (2000) *Age Speaks for Itself: Silent Voices of the Elderly*, Westport and London: Praeger.

Koren, M.J. (2010) 'Person-centered care for nursing home residents: The culture-change movement,' *Health Affairs*, 29(2), 312–317.

Levy, B., King, S., Hickey, L. and Hillary, M. (2017) *Spiritual Care in Residential Care Homes in Suffolk*, Ipswich: SIFRE.

Lodge, C., Carnell, E. and Coleman, M. (2016) *The New Age of Ageing: How Society Needs to Change*, Bristol: Policy Press.

Lutwack-Bloom, P., Wijewickrama R. and Smith, B. (2005) 'Effects of pets versus people visits with nursing home residents,' *Journal of Gerontological Social Work*, 44(3/4), 137–159.

MacKinlay, E. (2001) *The Spiritual Dimension of Ageing*, London: Jessica Kingsley Publishers.

MacKinlay, E. (2006) *Spiritual Growth and Care in the Fourth Age*, London: Jessica Kingsley Publishers.

McSherry, W. (2006) *Making Sense of Spirituality in Nursing and Health Care Practice*, London: Jessica Kingsley Publishers.

Making Leeds the Best City to Grow Old in: Annual Report 2017/2018, Leeds City Council.

Martin, B. (undated) *Buurtzorg Briefing Document*, London: Buurtzorg Britain and Ireland.

Maslow, A. (1943) 'A Theory of Human Motivation,' *Psychological Review*, 50(4), 370–396.

Matter Architecture (2019) *Rethinking Intergenerational Housing*, https://matterarchitecture.uk/intergen/

Matthews et al. (2013) *A Two-decade Comparison of Prevalence on Behalf of the Medical Research Council*, London: MRC.

'Moving from person-centred care to relationship-centred care' Partnerships in Dementia Care (accessed 2019) https://uwaterloo.ca/partnerships-in-dementia-care/sites/ca.partnerships-in-dementia-care/files/uploads/files/personcentredcare_vs_relationshipcentredcare_fact_sheet.pdf

Mowat, H. (2014) *The Promise of MHA Chaplaincy: A Journey towards Reconciliation and Restitution*, Derby: Methodist Homes Association.

Mowat, H. and Mowat, D. (2018) *The Freedom of Years: Ageing in Perspective*, Abingdon: BRF.

National Service Framework (NSF) for Older People (2001) Department of Health.

NHS Digital (2017) Personal Social Services Survey of Adult Carers in England, 2016–17. [Online] Available at: http://digital.nhs.uk/catalogue/PUB30045

Nolan, M.R. (2008) 'Relationship-centred care and the senses framework', *Journal of Dementia Care*, 16(1), 26–28.

Nolan, M.R., Brown, J., Davies, S., Nolan, J. and Keady, J. (2006). *The Senses Framework: Improving Care for Older People through a Relationship-centred Approach*, Getting Research into Practice (GRiP) Report No 2. Project Report, University of Sheffield.

O'Leary, M.F. et al. (2020) 'Evaluating the effect of a home-delivered meals service on the physical and psychological wellbeing of a UK population of older adults', *Journal of Nutrition in Gerontology and Geriatrics*, 39(1), 1–15. DOI:10.1080/21551197.2019.1684417

Orellana, K., Manthorpe, J. and Tinker, A. (2020) 'Day centres for older people – A systematically conducted scoping review of literature,' *Ageing and Society*, 40(1), 73–104. DOI: 10.1017/S0144686X18000843

Prince, M., et al. (2014) *Dementia UK: Update Second Edition*, London: Dementia UK.

Promoting Positive Mental Wellbeing for Older People: A Quick Guide for Registered Managers of Care Homes, (2020) Social Care Institute for Excellence.

Proud, L., McLoughlin, C. and Kinghorn, P. (2019) 'ICECAP-O, the current state of play: A systematic review of studies reporting the psychometric properties and use of the instrument over the decade since its publication,' *Quality of Life Research*, 28, 1429–1439.

Quinio, V. and Burgess, G. (2019) *Is Co-living a Housing Solution for Vulnerable Older People? Final Report*, Cambridge: Centre for Housing and Planning Research (University of Cambridge).

Reader, J. (2010) 'Wellbeing or resilience: Blurred encounters between theory and practice,' *The Practices of Happiness: Political Economy, Religion and Wellbeing*, edited by Atherton, Graham and Steedman, London: Routledge.

Rockwell, J. (2012) 'From personal-centred to relational care: Expanding the focus in residential care facilities,' *Journal of Gerontological Social Work*, 55(3), 233–248. DOI: 10.1080/01634372.2011.639438

Sayer, A. (2011) *Why Things Matter to People: Social Science, Values and Ethical Life*, Cambridge: Cambridge University Press.

Scott, P.A. (2017) *Key Concepts in Nursing Ethics*, London: Springer.

Sevenhuijsen, S. (1998) *Citizenship and the Ethics of Care: Feminist Considerations of Justice, Morality and Politics*, London: Routledge.

Sheard, D. (2013) *Mattering in a Dementia Care Home – The Butterfly Approach*, Brighton: Dementia Care Matters.

Somers, A. (2019) *The Intergenerational Programme at Nightingale House: A Study into the Impact on the Well-being of Elderly Residents, Executive Summary*. London: Nightingale Hammerson.

Storlie, T. (2015) *Person-Centered Communication with Older Adults*, London: Elsevier Academic Press.

Sumaya-Smith, I. (1995) Caregiver/resident relationships: surrogate family bonds and surrogate grieving in a skilled nursing facility. *Journal of Advanced Nursing*, 21(3), 447–451.

Swinton, J. (2001) *Spiritual Maturity in the Later Years*, New York: Howarth Pastoral Press.

Tanner, D. (2010) *Managing the Ageing Experience: Learning from Older People*, Bristol: The Policy Press.

Technology and Older People Evidence Review (2009, Age UK), https://www.ageuk.org.uk/Documents/EN-GB/For-professionals/Research/Evidence_Review_Technology.pdf?dtrk=true (accessed March 2020)

'"They remind me of my twins": How lifelike dolls are helping people with dementia, *The Guardian*, 22.1.20, https://www.theguardian.com/society/2020/jan/22/lifelike-dolls-dementia-care (accessed March 2020)

Tomlinson, J., Glenn, E., Paine, D. and Sandage, S. (2016) 'What is the "relational" in relational spirituality? A review of definitions and research directions', *Journal of Spirituality in Mental Health*, 18(1), 55–75.

Two Thirds of People Want Tax Increase to Pay for Health and Social Care, According to New Poll, (5 December 2019) The Health Foundation.

United for All ages (2020) *Together in the 2020s: Twenty Ideas for Creating a Britain for All Ages by 2030* (accessed March 2020) https://efeea61d-ae40-4f75-bfce-8a7be79f7237.filesusr.com/ugd/98d289_3f3291f2d4094c2793a3acf8ffaae58c.pd

Ward, E., Barnes, M., and Gahagan, B. (2012) *Well-being in Old Age: Findings from Participatory Research*, Brighton: SSPARC.

Watson, C. (2018) *The Language of Kindness: A Nurse's Story*, London: Vintage.

Whear, R. Thomson Coon, J. Bethel, A. Abbott, R. Stein, and Garside, R. (2014) 'What is the impact of using outdoor spaces such as gardens on the physical and mental well-being of those with dementia?'. *The Journal of Post-Acute and Long-term Care Medicine*, 15(10), 697–705.

WHO (2002) *Active Ageing: A Policy Framework*, Geneva: World Health Organisation.

Wilkinson, R.G. and Pickett, K. (2010) *The Spirit Level: Why Equality Is Better for Everyone*, London: Penguin.

Williams, F. (2004) *Rethinking Families*, London: Calouste Gulbenkian Foundation.

Woodward, J. and Kartupelis, J. (2018) *Developing a Relational Model of Care for Older People*, London: Jessica Kingsley Publishers.

Woodward, J. (2005) *Befriending Death*, London: SPCK.

Woodward, J. (2008) *Valuing Age: Pastoral Ministry with Older People*, London: New Library of Pastoral Care.

World Health Organisation (2007) *Global Age-Friendly Cities: A Guide*, Geneva: WHO Press.

York Consulting (2018) Evaluation of Neighbourhood Cares Pilot: Interim Report, Cambridge: Cambridgeshire County Council.

INDEX

For Product Safety Concerns and Information please contact our EU
representative GPSR@taylorandfrancis.com
Taylor & Francis Verlag GmbH, Kaufingerstraße 24, 80331 München, Germany

www.ingramcontent.com/pod-product-compliance
Lightning Source LLC
Chambersburg PA
CBHW070343270326
41926CB00017B/3958

9780367408541